the noodle cook book

the noodle cook book

Delicious recipes for crispy, stir-fried, boiled, sweet, spicy, hot and cold noodles

Kurumi Hayter

CHARTWELL
BOOKS, INC.

A QUINTET BOOK

Published by Chartwell Books
A Division of Book Sales, Inc.
114 Northfield Avenue
Edison, New Jersey 08837

This edition produced for sale in the U.S.A., its
territories and dependencies only.

ISBN 0-7858-0553-2

This book was designed and produced by
Quintet Publishing Limited
6 Blundell Street
London N7 9BH

Creative Director: **RICHARD DEWING**
Designer: **SIMON BALLEY**
Senior Editor: **LAURA SANDELSON**
Editor: **CAROLINE BALL**
Photographer: **DAVID ARMSTRONG**

Typeset in Great Britain by
Central Southern Typesetters, Eastbourne
Manufactured in Singapore by
Bright Arts (Pte) Ltd
Printed in Singapore by
Star Standard Industries (Pte) Ltd

DEDICATION
For my husband, Simon

contents

introduction

Above

Bunching noodles, Thailand

You will find them served from a stall by the roadside in the wastes of northern China, in crowded ramen shops in the heart of Tokyo's financial district, on the beach in the sandy resorts of Thailand, and in villages on the sub-tropical islands of Indonesia. In south and east Asia, the noodle is ubiquitous. In most Asian nations, it challenges rice as the main staple. Prepared in as little as five minutes, the humble noodle could even stake a claim to the title of the world's first and fastest fast food, though real noodle dishes bear no resemblance to the bland, anemic-looking strands lurking in pot noodle tubs on supermarket shelves. Noodles are never precooked, only prepared while you wait and served fresh and steaming hot. Noodles are nothing if not versatile. They can be made into a nourishing and filling meal accompanied by a broth to warm the coldest night, or made into a nest filled with stir-fried meat or vegetables for a hearty meal. They can be served as a salad, or over ice in a thin soy-based sauce as a refreshing summer treat. Noodles come in a wide range of types, thicknesses, and textures, from the delicate filaments of Thai vermicelli to finger-thick Japanese udon.

Noodles are high in carbohydrates, low in fat, and quickly prepared. With a high proportion of noodles and vegetables to animal products, they are a very healthy dietary alternative. With so much going for them, it is not surprising that noodles are beginning to catch on in a big way in the West. I hope reading this book will show you why.

Right

Noodles drying, China

types of noodles

There are close to twenty different varieties of noodles available, made from basic ingredients such as wheat, buckwheat, and rice flour. The different varieties require different treatment. Some noodles are best fried, while others make a better contribution boiled and served in a broth. Some can be made at home.

Soaking and cooking times given here are approximate, and may vary from brand to brand—check the instructions given on the package.

egg noodles

Egg noodles are made from wheat flour, egg, and water, and are eaten widely over southwest Asia both in soups and as stir-fried dishes. They commonly come in thin or medium thicknesses, and can be bought fresh or dried. Fresh egg noodles or fresh Japanese *ramen* noodles are best especially for hot noodle soups on account of their texture. Egg noodles can also be deep-fried to make crispy noodles. Japanese steamed noodles are especially suitable for stir-fried dishes. Fresh egg noodles are sold in Chinese stores, and fresh Japanese *ramen* noodles and steamed noodles are available from shops stocking Japanese foods. Other dried egg noodles are easily obtained from supermarkets.

Fresh and steamed egg noodles should be kept in the refrigerator (or freezer) and eaten within two or three days. Dried egg noodles can be kept over a long period as long as they are in an airtight package or container. Japanese fresh *ramen* or steamed noodles are often sold in a package with a ready-made soup or sauce.

cooking times

thin (fresh or dried) egg noodles

boil for 3 minutes

medium (fresh or dried) egg noodles

boil for 4 minutes

Japanese fresh *ramen*

boil for 2–3 minutes

Japanese steamed egg noodles

rinse in boiling water

udon, soba, and somen

Udon is mainly eaten in Japan and Korea, and are made from wheat flour and water. *Udon* noodles come in various thicknesses, both round and flat. *Udon* is sold at Chinese and Japanese supermarkets in fresh, parboiled, or dried forms. You can even make fresh *udon* at home (see page 24), but it requires professional skill to get exactly the right texture. It is suitable for hot noodle soups, cold dishes, and stir-fries.

Soba possesses its own distinctive flavor. It is made from buckwheat and plain flour, and is very nutritious, rich in protein and lecithin. *Soba* is sold fresh, parboiled, or dried at Japanese and Chinese stores, but hot dried *soba* is the most easy to find. It is served in hot noodle soups or as a cold dish.

Somen is made from wheat flour and water, and is only sold dried. Care should be taken handling *somen* as it is very fragile. *Somen* is commonly used for cold summer dishes, but can also be used in hot noodle soups.

cooking times

freshly made *udon*

boil for 13–15 minutes

parboiled fresh *udon*

boil for 3 minutes

flat *udon* (*kishimen*)

boil for 3–4 minutes

dried *udon*

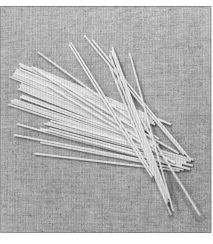

| boil for 7–15 minutes (depending on thickness) |

dried *soba*

| boil for 5–6 minutes |

somen

| boil for 1–2 minutes |

rice noodles

Rice vermicelli is made from rice flour and water, and is very fragile. It is sold in dried form at most supermarkets and Chinese stores. Rice vermicelli is deep-fried to make crispy noodles, and is also used in soups and stir-fries.

Rice-stick noodles (or *ho fun* in Chinese, *sen men* in Thai) vary in the thickness and shape. They are made from rice flour, starch, and water. Fresh steamed flat rice noodles are sold at Chinese supermarkets; these should be stored in the refrigerator and used within a couple of days of the purchase.

soaking times

rice vermicelli

| 3–5 minutes in warm water |

rice-stick noodles

| 2–5 minutes in warm water |

fresh steamed flat rice noodles

| rinse with hot water |

bean-thread noodles

Bean-thread vermicelli or noodles, also known as transparent, cellophane, or mung bean-thread noodles, are made from mung bean flour. They are sold at Chinese stores in dried form, and look similar to rice vermicelli. However, these noodles are tougher than rice vermicelli, and are used for soups, delicate stews, braised dishes, and in stir-fries.

soaking time

bean-thread vermicelli

5 minutes in boiling water

Right

Eating ("slurping") noodles, Xinjiang, China

How to prepare and cook noodles

Cooking noodles is simplicity itself. All that is needed is a large pan of water. The essential thing about noodles, like spaghetti, is to get the texture right, which means that care should be taken to avoid overcooking. Timing is another important consideration. The other elements of the dish should all be ready so that once the noodles are cooked everything can be served without delay, as cooked noodles tend to stick together if left for any time after cooking.

boiling method

ramen and egg noodles
Bring plenty of water to a boil in a pan, then add the noodles. Stir a couple of times to prevent the noodles sticking together.

udon and soba

Bring plenty of water to a boil in a pan. Add the *udon* or *soba,* and stir a couple of times. When the water is about to boil, add a small cup of water to bring the temperature down. When the water comes back to the boil, add more water. Rinse well under cold water, and drain.

somen

As with egg noodles and *udon,* the only thing you need is boiling water. Immerse the *somen,* and stir a couple of times. When the water is coming to the boil, add a small cup of water only once. As the water is about to boil over, it is ready. Rinse well under cold water.

soaking method

Rice noodles need to be soaked in warm water, while bean thread noodles are soaked in boiling water. Both types of noodles are then rinsed with cold water and drained. The soaking time varies according to the type and thickness of the noodles (refer to the instructions on the package).

Above Left

Boiling egg

noodles

Above

Right

Deep-frying

rice

vermicelli

deep-frying (to make crispy noodles)

egg noodles

First boil in hot water (see above), then rinse and drain. The noodles should then be separated, spread out on a tray, and dried well. Heat the oil to 350°F and fry small amounts at a time, using chopsticks or tongs to turn them. Deep-fry until the noodles turn a golden brown. When cooked, they should be drained on paper towels.

rice vermicelli

Rice vermicelli can be deep-fried without any preparation. Fry only small amounts at a time. After only a few seconds the vermicelli becomes puffy and white; take it out and drain on paper towels.

serving and eating noodles

Noodles absorb liquid very rapidly, which is why it is essential not to overcook them. By the same token, it is important that hot noodle soup dishes are served and eaten as soon as they are ready. So only pour the broth over noodles just before you are going to eat them. Don't worry about making a slurping sound when eating noodles; it is not only unavoidable, but part of the fun!

note

All recipes are for four servings unless indicated otherwise.
Ingredients not strictly necessary are listed as (optional).
Spoon measures are level.

utensils

*T*he utensils for cooking noodles are basic and all derived from the Chinese kitchen. One of the most useful and simple pieces of equipment to have on hand is a wok. This versatile pan can be used for stir-frying, deep-frying, braising, boiling, and steaming. The wok is traditionally made from iron, though modern nonstick versions are also available. If you do not own a wok, a large, deep frying pan can be used as a substitute.

how to care for a wok

After use, the wok should be scrubbed well with a brush in hot water. Do not use dishwashing liquid as the wok's surface should remain oily in order to prevent rusting. After hand drying, return the wok to the stove for about a minute, to dry the surface thoroughly. When dry, dip a paper towel in a little oil and wipe the inside of the wok as a further preventative against rusting. Only when a wok has become rusty should you use dishwashing liquid.

using a wok

The wok should be heated before oil is added. To be hot enough for stir-frying, the oil should be heated until it begins to smoke, which prevents the ingredients from sticking to the wok.

Below *Two designs of wok, one with the traditional long wooden handle and the other with two carrying handles. The brush may be used to oil woks, and the strainers are useful accessories for some recipes*

techniques
and
preparation

"Chopstick cultures" demand that most food be chopped or sliced into bite-sized pieces before cooking. Usually, all ingredients, whether they be meat, fish, or vegetable, are cut into the same size. As the origins of the noodle stem from Chinese cuisine, most noodle-based dishes follow this basic precept, even though the fork and spoon are used in place of chopsticks in countries such as Thailand and Indonesia.

Left Most noodle dishes require ingredients to be chopped or sliced in order to facilitate easy eating with chopsticks

cutting techniques

fine chopping

The meat or vegetable is first thinly sliced, then chopped very finely into a mince.

dicing

Vegetables and *tofu* are cut thickly, then cut again into small cubes.

random cutting

Vegetables are cut and rolled at the same time in order to produce the random effect.

matchsticks

Vegetables are cut into matchstick-sized pieces.

shredding

Vegetables are thinly sliced first, then shredded more finely than matchsticks.

diagonal slicing

Vegetables are sliced thinly on a slant. This technique is often used before shredding.

slanted cutting

It is not easy to cut meat into fine slices by yourself. If your butcher will not do this for you, the easiest method is as follows. Half-freeze the meat, then cut, slanting the knife in the direction of the cut to get the thinnest slices.

glossary

Bamboo shoots When bamboo has just appeared above the ground, it is edible and collected in large quantities. Fresh bamboo shoots are widely used in oriental countries. Parboiled and canned bamboo shoots are widely available. Sliced canned bamboo shoots are used in this book. Cooked dried bamboo shoots (*shinachiku*) originated in China, but are now frequently used as a garnish for *ramen* dishes in Japan. *Shinachiku* is available from Japanese stores.

Bean curd (*tofu*) Bean curd is made from soya beans and has a soft texture. It is a very healthy food, high in protein and low in fat. There are two types available, firm cotton *tofu* and fragile silken *tofu*. Cotton *tofu* is used in this book, and is widely available from large supermarkets, healthfood shops, and oriental food shops. If you cannot use it all, immerse the *tofu* in water in a container and store it in the refrigerator, where it will last a few days. The water must be changed daily.

Bean curd sheet (*abura-age*) *Abura-age* is a sheet of deep-fried bean curd, also made from soybeans. It is used in Japanese cooking, and can be obtained from Japanese grocers. Do not confuse it with Chinese dried bean curd. Before use, always rinse it with hot water to wash off any excess oil. *Abura-age* can be frozen.

Black bean sauce Black beans are salted and fermented with spices to produce this sauce. It has a strong, salty taste, and is used widely in southeast Asian and Chinese cooking. Black bean sauce is available at supermarkets and oriental grocers; the taste can vary depending on the brand.

Bonito flakes (*katuso-bushi*) Bonito is a member of the tuna family. When dried and grated into flakes, it is one of the essential ingredients in Japanese cuisine. It is mainly used for making Japanese broth, but also as an ingredient in other dishes and as a garnish. Available from Japanese grocers, large supermarkets, and healthfood shops. Keep it stored in an airtight container.

Bowles' mint (*oba*) The leaves of the *oba* plant are large, round, and mid-green, and taste of spearmint. Fresh *oba* leaves are used extensively for mixing with other ingredients, or as a garnish. They are available at Japanese grocers.

Candle nut Round candle nuts are the fruit of the candleberry tree. They are used crushed or ground as thickening agents with other ingredients. Macadamia nuts can be used as a fine substitute.

***Cha siu* sauce** This is the marinade sauce used for making Chinese barbecued pork. It is a blend of many ingredients, including Chinese five spices, honey, sugar, soy sauce, rice wine, and garlic. *Cha siu* sauce is sold at oriental stores.

Chile bean sauce (*toban djan*) *Toban djan* is a thick, dark reddish sauce, made from chili, soy beans, and soy sauce. It is used for spicing up Chinese dishes. Chile bean sauce is available from large supermarkets or oriental food stores.

Chile oil Chile oil is a red-colored oil, made from ground chile peppers. It is used for cooking, as a spice, and can be added to some dips. Chile oil is available from supermarkets as well as from oriental grocers.

Chile sauce (*sambal oelek*) *Sambal oelek* is an Indonesian chile paste, made from crushed red chiles. It is used for cooking as well as a condiment. *Sambal oelek* is sold at Asian grocers.

Chinese green chives These are leafy stems about 12 inches long. As a substitute, the green stem section of scallions can be used. Chinese green chives are sold at Chinese grocers.

chili oil

oba

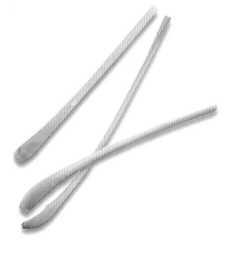

lemon grass

Chinese rice wine There are several kinds of rice wine, the most famous of which is *Shaoxing*, used for drinking and cooking. In this book, clear rice wine is used.

Coconut milk Coconut milk is a thick cream made from coconut flesh, not the watery fluid from the middle of a fresh coconut. It is available canned or in powder form, and quality varies. It is sold at large supermarkets, Asian shops, and Indian grocers.

Crispy onion/fried onion Thinly sliced onion shallow-fried until brown and crisp is not easy to make at home, but is sold in supermarkets and oriental grocers. It is used as a garnish.

Daikon or mooli Daikon is a long, white radish, also known as *mooli* in the West. It is eaten raw, just grated, or cooked. *Mooli* is a slightly narrower radish, and is easier to obtain.

Dried black ear fungus A mushroom used in Chinese dishes, black ear fungus are usually sold dried and have to be soaked in warm water before use; it expands to about four times its dried size. It has a firm texture. Dried black ear fungus is sold at oriental grocers.

Dried kelp (konbu) Konbu, dark strips of kelp, is one of the most essential ingredients for making Japanese broth. It is usually dried and dark green in color. It should be wiped with a damp cloth before use. *Konbu* is available from large supermarkets, healthfood stores, and Japanese stores.

Dried baby shrimp Do not confuse these with dried shrimp paste; dried baby shrimp are salty, hard, whole shrimp, used for adding extra flavor. Sometimes they are soaked in water before use. Dried baby shrimp are very different from the Japanese variety. You can find them in Chinese and Thai food stores.

Dried shrimp paste (belacan) Belacan is a fermented shrimp paste with a very characteristic, strong smell. Before use, *belacan* has to be fried. It is sold at Chinese and Thai grocers.

Enoki mushrooms Enoki mushrooms are slender, creamy in color with tiny caps. They grow from a dense set of roots, which must be cut off prior to use. *Enoki* mushrooms are available from Japanese and Chinese stores.

Fish balls Fish balls are made from pounded fish paste, and are slightly smaller than golf balls.

Fish sauce (nam pla) Nam pla is a light brown liquid made from salted, fermented fish. It is one of the essential seasonings in Thai cuisine, and has a seaside, fishy smell. *Nam pla* is sold at oriental grocers.

Galangal Galangal is a cousin of ginger; it is slightly harder, the aroma is a little different, and it is not as pungent. Fresh ginger may be substituted, but use half the amount.

Gobo Gobo is a narrow, long, edible root akin to the burdock. When using fresh, scrape with a knife and soak in vinegared water to prevent discoloration. It is full of fiber and used in Japanese cooking; it is available from Japanese grocers.

Japanese fermented soybeans (natto) Natto is the end product of fermenting soy beans. It is very sticky, and has a smell that some find offputting. It is not every Japanese's favorite, but is very good for you, being high in fiber and protein.

Japanese fish cake (kamaboko) Kamaboko is a Japanese version of a fish cake. It is made from pulped white fish gelled into a firm, semi-cylindrical shape. It is mainly eaten sliced, accompanied by soy sauce.

miso

dried baby shrimp

Japanese fermented soybeans (natto)

Japanese rice wine (sake) The taste of Japanese rice wine is very different from its Chinese equivalent. *Sake* is made from fermented steamed rice, water, and enzyme, and tastes sweeter. It is used for both cooking and drinking. *Sake* is sold in large supermarkets, some liquor stores, and oriental stores.

Kaffir lime leaves Kaffir lime leaves are widely used as a flavoring in Thai cuisine, and also used in some Malaysian and Indonesian dishes. They are sold fresh or dried at Asian grocers and large supermarkets.

Lemon grass Lemon grass is used in Thai, Malay, and Indonesian cooking to add the flavor of citrus to dishes. it is sold at supermarkets and Asian grocers.

Mirin Made from rice, water, and alcohol (but with a low alcohol content), *Mirin* is used to enhance sweetness in Japanese cooking. It is sold at Japanese and Chinese grocers.

Miso paste *Miso* paste is another soy product, made from fermented cooked soybeans. It is very salty, and is frequently used in Japanese cuisine. There are two types of *miso*, white and red. In this book, red *miso* is used as it has a stronger flavor than the mild, white version. *Miso* is sold in large supermarkets, healthfood stores, and oriental grocers. It should be stored in the refrigerator, where it will last for several months.

Chinese mushrooms (nameko)

Mustard greens Mustard greens are used for Chinese dishes. Fresh mustard greens are available from Chinese grocers, or spinach can be used as a substitute.

Myoga *Myoga* is a relation of the ginger plant. It is the *myoga* buds that are eaten, either raw, pickled, or as a garnish in Japanese dishes.

Nameko mushrooms *Nameko* mushrooms are small with light brown caps and have a slippery outer coating.

Nori *Nori* is blackish-green laver seaweed dried into paper-thin sheets. Some *nori* must be heated in a skillet for a few seconds, until the color of the *nori* changes to green. *Nori* should be kept in an airtight container and handled with care as it flakes easily. It is sold at large supermarkets, healthfood shops, and oriental food shops.

Oyster sauce Oyster sauce is made from extract of oysters, salt, and soy sauce. Oyster sauce has a characteristic smell, and is often used for flavoring dishes in Chinese cuisine. It is sold in supermarkets and oriental grocers.

Palm sugar Made from the sap of the coconut palm, palm sugar or jaggery is used throughout southeast Asia. It is light brown, and has a sweet caramel smell. Palm sugar is available from Asian shops, or brown sugar can be used as a substitute.

Red pickled ginger (beni-shouga) Slivered ginger is pickled with a little sugar and vinegar and used as a garnish in Japanese dishes. It is sold at Japanese grocers.

nori

Satoimo *Satoimo* is a potato with dark brown, hairy skin. The flesh is white and slippery. To prepare, wash with a brush under running water, and then peel—wear gloves as the flesh can cause an itching sensation. *Satoimo* is a common ingredient in Japanese cooking. It is sold in large supermarkets and oriental grocers.

Sesame oil Sesame oil is made from sesame seeds and has a distinctive aroma. It is used as a flavoring and is easily available.

Sesame paste/sauce Made from pounded sesame seeds and a creamy light brown in color, sesame paste has an aromatic smell. Peanut butter can be used as a substitute, but sesame paste is available from large supermarkets or oriental grocers.

Seven flavors chili powder (shichimi) *Shichimi* is a Japanese chili powder, ground and blended with a mixture of red chile pepper, black pepper, sesame seeds, poppy seeds, *nori*, hemp seeds, and *sansho* pepper. It is used as a seasoning over *udon* or *soba* noodle soup and other Japanese dishes. *Shichimi* is sold at Japanese and Chinese grocers.

Shiitake mushrooms *Shiitake* mushrooms are widely used in oriental cooking. They have a characteristic smoky smell, especially after soaking. Soak dried mushrooms in warm water for about 20 minutes, and remove the stems. Fresh mushrooms are available in season from supermarkets, healthfood shops, and oriental food stores.

seven-flavors chili powder

Shimeji mushrooms *Shimeji* mushrooms grow in short, stumpy clusters from a simple root. The stalks are creamy at the base, gradually becoming grayish brown toward the cap. They have a mild, subtle flavor, and form a frequent ingredient in Japanese cooking. Cut off the root before use. They can be obtained from Japanese stores.

Soured plums (umeboshi) *Umeboshi* are green plums that have been salted with red *shiso* leaves, and are a traditional Japanese preserved food. They taste very sour, so a little goes a long way. Some Japanese still make *umeboshi* at home. They are sold in cartons in Japanese grocers.

Soy sauce Many countries in Asia produce their own soy sauce, made from soybeans, salt, wheat flour, and water first fermented and then brewed. Three kinds of soy sauce are used in this book:
Japanese soy sauce: similar to light soy sauce, though less salty.
Light soy sauce: a Chinese product, very salty and used frequently for flavoring.
Dark soy sauce: much darker than the other two as it is aged longer. It is less salty, and has a hint of sweetness.

All these soy sauces are widely available.

Straw mushrooms Straw mushrooms are oval in shape with dark brown caps, and are used as ingredients in Chinese and other Oriental cuisines. They are sold canned in large supermarkets and oriental grocers.

Tamarind Dried tamarind pulp is first soaked in water, then strained to squeeze out the dark juice. It is used to sour southeast Asian food as well as Indian dishes. Tamarind pulp is sold at Indian and Asian grocers.

Thai red curry paste Red curry paste is made from the combination of red chiles, lemon grass, shallots, garlic, shrimp paste, *galangal*, coriander, fennel, and other spices. It has a hot but sour taste quite distinct from Indian curry. Thai curry paste is sold in large supermarkets and Asian food shops.

Wakame seaweed *Wakame* is a green seaweed, thinner than kelp (*konbu*), and is used in Japanese cooking. Dried *wakame* must be soaked in water for 5 minutes or in hot water for 2 minutes before use. It is easier to store and more readily available, (from large supermarkets, healthfood shops, and Japanese grocers), than fresh salted *wakame*.

Wasabi *Wasabi* is a Japanese horseradish that grows only in clean water; it is the pungent root that is edible. Fresh *wasabi* is grated and used as a garnish, but even in Japan it is expensive and difficult to purchase. *Wasabi* powder or paste is commonly used and available from Japanese and Chinese grocers.

Water chestnuts The water chestnut is actually a bulb, very similar in shape to a chestnut but unrelated. Water chestnuts have a crunchy texture and are used in Chinese dishes. Peeled, white water chestnuts are easily available canned in large supermarkets and oriental grocers.

Wonton wrappers Wonton wrappers are paper-thin, small square sheets made from flour, egg, and water. They are used for wrapping a filling of ground meat, vegetables, or shrimp, then fried, steamed, or boiled in soup. Wontons originated in China, but are also widely eaten in other Asian countries. Fresh or frozen wonton wrappers are available from Chinese grocers.

Yakisoba sauce *Yakisoba* sauce is a dark brown sauce, used in Japanese stir-fried noodles. Japanese brown sauce is a good substitute, or blend your own *yakisoba* sauce from the recipe on page 88. *Yakisoba* sauce and Japanese brown sauce are sold at Japanese grocers.

Yam (yama-imo) The yam is a relation of the sweet potato. It varies in shape and size, and is white in color. When peeled, the yam begins to ooze and become sticky, so when you grate it, expose only a small amount of the flesh at a time.

Yellow bean sauce Made from fermented yellow beans with flour and salt, yellow bean sauce is used in Chinese cooking. It is thick and salty, but with a hint of sweetness. Yellow bean sauce is sold in jars in supermarkets and oriental grocers.

wasabi

wakame seaweed

hot noodle soups

Hot noodle soups make for warm bodies on cold windy days. Ramen *is the Japanese name for Chinese noodles. Thai, Malaysian, and Indonesian noodle soups are entirely different from Chinese and Japanese hot noodle soups—a spicy, sour taste dominates their broth, and chile is one of the most important ingredients. Udon and soba are mainly eaten in Japan. Once you have a good stock for these hot noodle recipes, you are halfway toward producing a delicious, wholesome dish.*

making fresh *udon*

Making udon *noodles is usually a professional job in Japan, and both fresh and dried* udon *are widely available in the shops. A key point to successful homemade* udon *is good, hard kneading. If you cannot bring yourself to use your feet and tread on the dough, you can knead by hand. Just make sure you knead well. When you knead the dough with your feet, remember to take off your shoes! The texture of freshly made* udon *is firm and entirely different from dried* udon. *Boiling time for freshly made* udon *is 14–15 minutes. They can be refrigerated in a plastic bag for up to three days.*

1. Adding water to flour

2. Kneading *udon* into a round

3. Slicing *udon* into strips

making fresh udon

2 tbsp salt
1 cup water
4 cups self-rising flour
flour for dusting

● Dissolve the salt in the water in a cup. Sift the flour into a large bowl. Add the salted water little by little, mixing with chopsticks or a fork. Then, with your fingers, mix to a fine breadcrumb consistency.

● Knead with your hands, and then form the dough into a round. Wrap with a wet cloth and leave for 30–60 minutes. Dust your worktop with flour, knead again, shape into a round, and put into a thick plastic bag. Using your feet, knead the dough strongly for 10 minutes.

● Remove the dough from the bag. Dust the worktop with flour, and roll the dough out to a thickness of ¼ in. Dust with flour again, then fold the dough, so you can slice it easily into ¼-in strips.

basic stocks

For many noodle dishes, a good stock is essential for success since it is the stock that lends flavor to the dish. Basic stocks are easily prepared if somewhat time-consuming, but once the stock is prepared, noodle soups can be made quickly and simply. Most Asian countries have their own preferred types of stock. When you make a stock, it is wise to make more than you need at any one time since you can keep stock in the refrigerator for a few days, or freeze for later use. If you have no time to prepare your own, instant stocks are available from oriental food stockists.

chicken stock

Makes 7–8 cups

Used to make Chinese and *Ramen* hot noodle soups and Chinese sauces. Pork bones can be replaced with more chicken bones if wished.

1¼ lb chicken bones, chopped roughly
¼ lb pork bones
I small onion, cut in half
I small leek, cut in half diagonally
2 fat cloves garlic, lightly crushed
I-inch piece fresh ginger, peeled and sliced
10 cups water

● Wash the bones before use. Blanch the chicken and pork bones in boiling water for 2 minutes. Rinse.
● Put the bones, onion, leek, garlic, ginger, and water in a large pan. Bring to a boil, then simmer for 1 hour, skimming off the scum occasionally. After an hour, strain the stock through a fine mesh strainer or cheesecloth.

light chicken stock

Makes about 6 cups

Used for Thai, Malaysian, and Indonesian hot noodle dishes.

7½ cups water
3 chicken drumsticks

● Put the water and chicken drumsticks in a saucepan, bring to a boil, and simmer for about 40 minutes. When the meat on the drumstick shin begins to fall away, exposing the bone, the stock should be ready. Strain through a metal sieve, and reserve the drumstick meat as a topping for a noodle dish.

miso broth

Makes 6 cups

I tbsp sesame oil
½-inch piece fresh ginger, peeled and finely chopped
I clove garlic, finely chopped
I scallion, finely chopped
4 tbsp Chinese rice wine or Japanese *sake*
3 tbsp light soy sauce
2 tbsp sugar
8 tbsp red *miso* paste
2 tsp chile oil
6 cups chicken stock
black pepper

● Heat the oil in a pan. Add the ginger, garlic, and scallion, then fry for 30 seconds. Add the wine first, then soy sauce, sugar, *miso* paste, and chile oil, and mix together. Add the chicken stock, and bring to a boil. Remove from the heat, and the broth is now ready to use.

Left *Ingredients for vegetable stock*

soy sauce broth

Makes 6 cups

6 cups chicken stock (*see page 25*)
2 tsp salt
4 tsp Chinese rice wine or Japanese sake
2 tsp shortening
4 tbsp light soy sauce
4 tsp dark soy sauce
black pepper

● Put the stock, salt, wine, and shortening in a pan. Bring to a boil, and simmer for 2–3 minutes. Turn off the heat, add the light and dark soy sauce, black pepper, and stir. The broth is now ready to use.

vegetable stock

Makes about 4½ cups

For vegetarians, vegetable stock can be substituted for chicken stock.

I tbsp vegetable oil
I fat clove garlic, sliced
I-inch piece fresh ginger, sliced
½ leek, sliced
I carrot, chopped
I medium-sized onion, chopped
I½ stalks celery, chopped
5 cups water

● Heat the oil in a saucepan and fry all the vegetables for 2 minutes. Add the water, bring to a boil, and simmer for 40 minutes. Strain through a metal sieve.

premier Japanese dashi

Makes about 6 cups

Used for making Japanese broth.

6 cups water
4-inch piece dried kelp (konbu), wiped with a damp cloth
3 cups bonito flakes (katsuo-bushi)

● First, make two or three cuts about I inch long in the kelp to release more flavor, then put the water and kelp in a saucepan and heat under a low flame. Remove the kelp just before the water begins to boil. Add the bonito flakes when the liquid comes back to the boil, and turn off the heat. Leave the liquid until the flakes sink to the bottom of the pan, then sieve through a cheesecloth or paper filter. Retain the bonito flakes and kelp for preparing standard *dashi*.

standard dashi

Makes about 6 cups

This recipe recycles bonito flakes and kelp used in making Premier Japanese Dashi. It is used in the same way.

6 cups water
used kelp and bonito flakes from premier dashi

● Put the water, kelp, and bonito flakes in a large saucepan. Bring to the boil over a low heat, and simmer for about 5 minutes. Skim off any scum that forms on the surface. Sieve through cheesecloth or a coffee filter.

dashi broth

kake-tsuyu
Makes about 6 cups

2 tbsp mirin
6 cups premier dashi
scant ½ cup Japanese soy sauce
3 tbsp sugar

● Put the *mirin* in a saucepan, and bring to a boil. Add the *dashi*, soy sauce, and sugar, then simmer for about 3–4 minutes. It is now ready to use.

dipping broth

tsuke-tsuyu
Makes about 3 cups

¾ cup mirin
2¼ cups premier dashi
¾ cup Japanese soy sauce

● Put the *mirin* in a saucepan, and bring to a boil. Add the *dashi* and soy sauce and simmer for 3–4 minutes; then remove from the heat and chill in the refrigerator.
● Dipping broth can be stored refrigerated in a jar for 3–4 days.

hot and sour noodle soup with shrimp

tom yam goong with rice vermicelli

Tom yam goong is one of the representative dishes of Thai cuisine. The broth is a myriad of flavors: the sour element of lime leaves and lemon grass combined with the hot chile pepper and *nam pla*, with its strong seafood aroma.

1 tbsp vegetable oil
2 cloves garlic, grated
2 shallots, grated
1-inch piece *galangal*, or ½ inch fresh ginger, thinly sliced
4–5 small red chiles, chopped
6 cups light chicken stock *(see page 25)*
3 Kaffir lime leaves, sliced
4-inch piece lemon grass, chopped
½ lb rice vermicelli
20 peeled tiger shrimp
6 tbsp fish sauce (*nam pla*)
6 tbsp fresh lemon or lime juice
2 tbsp palm or brown sugar
16 canned straw mushrooms
cilantro leaves

● Heat the oil in a saucepan, then stir-fry the garlic, shallots, *galangal,* and chile for about 1 minute. Put in the chicken stock, add the lime leaves and lemon grass, bring to a boil, and simmer for 5 minutes.

● Meanwhile, soak the rice vermicelli for 3 minutes, rinse, drain, and divide into four bowls. Add the shrimp, fish sauce, lemon or lime juice, sugar, and straw mushrooms to the soup, then simmer for 2–3 minutes.

● Pour the soup into the bowls and sprinkle with the cilantro leaves. Serve immediately.

hot and sour noodle soup with chicken

tom yam with rice vermicelli

This is another hot and sour Thai noodle soup. The authentic Thai version blends ferocious heat with refreshing sourness. I have not used as much chile in this recipe, but I assure you it is still plenty hot!

1 tbsp vegetable oil
2 cloves garlic, finely chopped
2 shallots, finely chopped
1-inch piece *galangal,* or ½-inch
  fresh ginger, thinly sliced
5–6 small red chiles, chopped
4 cups light chicken stock *(see page 25)*
3 Kaffir lime leaves, sliced
2-inch piece lemon grass, sliced
½ lb rice vermicelli
6 tbsp fish sauce (*nam pla*)
6 tbsp fresh lemon juice
2 tsp palm or brown sugar
16 canned straw mushrooms
chicken meat from the light
  chicken stock, thinly sliced
1 large lettuce leaf, shredded
cilantro leaves

● Heat the oil in a saucepan; stir-fry the garlic, shallots, *galangal,* and chile for 2 minutes. Add the chicken stock, lime leaves, and lemon grass. Bring to a boil, and simmer for 5 minutes.
● Soak the rice vermicelli in warm water, rinse, and drain. Put the vermicelli into four bowls. Add the fish sauce, lemon juice, sugar, straw mushrooms, and chicken meat to the soup and simmer for 2–3 minutes.
● Add the lettuce and cilantro, then simmer for 1 minute. Pour the soup into the bowls, and serve immediately.

creamy coconut noodle soup

laksa lemak

A famous Malaysian dish reflecting the multicultural nature of that country and its people. *Laksa lemak* should be treated with caution. Eat it once, and you will be hopelessly addicted to its smooth texture and silky hot taste!

8 shallots, sliced
3 cloves garlic, sliced
2-inch piece *galangal,* or 1-inch
  ginger, peeled and sliced
4 small red chiles, sliced
1 tbsp chopped fresh lemon
  grass
5 tbsp vegetable oil
2 tsp ground turmeric
1 tsp ground coriander
2 tsp dried shrimp paste
  (*belacan*) (optional)
¼ lb bean curd (*tofu*), diced
2¼ cups light chicken stock *(see page 25)*
2 cups coconut milk
2 tsp sugar
2 tsp salt
2 fish balls, or 2 golfball-sized
  chunks imitation crabmeat,
  sliced
½ lb rice vermicelli
12 tiger or large shrimp, peeled
  and deveined
For the garnish:
  cooked chicken from the light
  chicken stock, shredded
1½ cups bean sprouts
2-inch piece cucumber,
  shredded
1 large red chile, sliced
2 scallions, chopped

● Blend the shallots, garlic, *galangal,* red chile, and lemon grass in a food processor. Heat 3 tablespoons of the oil in a saucepan, and stir-fry the shallot mixture with the turmeric, coriander seeds, and dried shrimp paste over a low heat for 3–4 minutes
● Heat the remaining oil in a frying pan, and fry the bean curd until lightly browned. Add the chicken stock, coconut milk, sugar, salt, and fish balls or imitation crabmeat, bring to a boil, and simmer for 2–3 minutes.
● Meanwhile, blanch the bean sprouts in boiling water for 1 minute. Soak the vermicelli in warm water for 3 minutes, rinse, and drain well. Divide the vermicelli into four bowls.
● Add the shrimp to the soup, and simmer for 2 minutes. Pour the soup into the bowls; garnish with shredded chicken, bean sprouts, cucumber, sliced chile, and scallions. Serve immediately.

Right
Creamy Coconut Noodle Soup

Malaysian sour noodle soup

laksa penang

This is a version of *laksa lemak* from Penang. The stock is made from fish, and coconut milk is not used. The soup has a spicy, sour taste.

I lb cod
7 cups water
4 shallots, sliced
2 cloves garlic, sliced
2-inch piece *galangal,* or 1-inch
 ginger, chopped
3 small red chiles, chopped
2-inch stalk lemon grass
2 tbsp vegetable oil
2 tsp ground turmeric
2 tsp dried shrimp paste
 (*belacan*) (optional)
4 tbsp tamarind pulp
2 tsp salt
2 tsp sugar
½ lb rice vermicelli
For the garnish:
1½ cups bean sprouts
2 rings canned pineapple,
 chopped
2-inch piece cucumber,
 shredded
3 fresh Kaffir lime leaves, sliced
 mint leaves, sliced
I large red chile, sliced

● Put the cod and water in a saucepan, bring to a boil, and simmer for 15–20 minutes. Meanwhile, blend the shallots, garlic, *galangal,* small red chiles, and lemon grass in a mixer or food processor.
● When the fish stock is ready, take out the fish, remove the skin, and flake the meat. Heat the oil in saucepan, then fry the shallot mixture with the ground turmeric and dried shrimp paste for 3–4 minutes.

● Soak the tamarind pieces in warm water for 5 minutes, then sieve to squeeze and extract the juice. Add the fish stock, fish flakes, salt, sugar, and tamarind juice to the fried spice mixture in the pan, and simmer for 3–4 minutes.
● Soak the rice vermicelli in warm water for 3 minutes, rinse, and drain. Put into four bowls. Blanch the bean sprouts in boiling water for 1 minute.
● Pour the fish soup into serving bowls. Garnish with the bean sprouts, pineapple, cucumber, lime leaves, mint leaves, and red chile. Serve at once.

Indonesian chicken soup with rice vermicelli

soto ayam

This Indonesian soup dish has a spicy, sour, and nutty flavor. *Sambal oelek* provides the spice in this soup. If you like a hotter taste, simply add more.

2 tbsp vegetable oil
4 shallots, sliced
3 cloves garlic, sliced
2-inch piece *galangal,* or 1-inch
 fresh ginger, sliced
I tsp ground coriander
3 tbsp candle or macadamia
 nuts
6 cups light chicken stock (*see
 page 25*)
2 tsp salt
cooked chicken meat from the
 light chicken stock, shredded
½ lb rice vermicelli

For the topping:
2 tsp salt
1½ cups bean sprouts, blanched
2 scallions, chopped
I stalk celery, sliced
2 tbsp ready-made crispy
 onions
4 lime wedges
2 tsp Indonesian chile paste
 (*sambal oelek*) or chile sauce

● Heat the oil in a frying pan. Fry the shallots, garlic, galangal or ginger, and the ground coriander, then add the nuts. Blend to a paste with 3 tablespoons chicken stock in a mixer or food processor.
● Put the paste and chicken stock in a pan, and simmer for 5 minutes. Then add the chicken meat and salt, and simmer for 2–3 minutes. Meanwhile, soak the rice vermicelli in warm water for 3 minutes. Rinse, drain, and divide into four bowls.
● Put the bean sprouts, scallions, and celery on top of the noodles. Pour the soup in, and sprinkle with the crispy onions. Garnish with lime wedges and half a teaspoon of chile sauce to each bowl. Serve immediately.

Malaysian sour noodle soup

laksa penang

This is a version of *laksa lemak* from Penang. The stock is made from fish, and coconut milk is not used. The soup has a spicy, sour taste.

1 lb cod
7 cups water
4 shallots, sliced
2 cloves garlic, sliced
2-inch piece *galangal,* or 1-inch ginger, chopped
3 small red chiles, chopped
2-inch stalk lemon grass
2 tbsp vegetable oil
2 tsp ground turmeric
2 tsp dried shrimp paste (*belacan*) (optional)
4 tbsp tamarind pulp
2 tsp salt
2 tsp sugar
½ lb rice vermicelli
For the garnish:
1½ cups bean sprouts
2 rings canned pineapple, chopped
2-inch piece cucumber, shredded
3 fresh Kaffir lime leaves, sliced
mint leaves, sliced
1 large red chile, sliced

● Put the cod and water in a saucepan, bring to a boil, and simmer for 15–20 minutes. Meanwhile, blend the shallots, garlic, *galangal*, small red chiles, and lemon grass in a mixer or food processor.

● When the fish stock is ready, take out the fish, remove the skin, and flake the meat. Heat the oil in saucepan, then fry the shallot mixture with the ground turmeric and dried shrimp paste for 3–4 minutes.

● Soak the tamarind pieces in warm water for 5 minutes, then sieve to squeeze and extract the juice. Add the fish stock, fish flakes, salt, sugar, and tamarind juice to the fried spice mixture in the pan, and simmer for 3–4 minutes.

● Soak the rice vermicelli in warm water for 3 minutes, rinse, and drain. Put into four bowls. Blanch the bean sprouts in boiling water for 1 minute.

● Pour the fish soup into serving bowls. Garnish with the bean sprouts, pineapple, cucumber, lime leaves, mint leaves, and red chile. Serve at once.

Indonesian chicken soup with rice vermicelli

soto ayam

This Indonesian soup dish has a spicy, sour, and nutty flavor. *Sambal oelek* provides the spice in this soup. If you like a hotter taste, simply add more.

2 tbsp vegetable oil
4 shallots, sliced
3 cloves garlic, sliced
2-inch piece *galangal,* or 1-inch fresh ginger, sliced
1 tsp ground coriander
3 tbsp candle or macadamia nuts
6 cups light chicken stock (*see page 25*)
2 tsp salt
cooked chicken meat from the light chicken stock, shredded
½ lb rice vermicelli

For the topping:
2 tsp salt
1½ cups bean sprouts, blanched
2 scallions, chopped
1 stalk celery, sliced
2 tbsp ready-made crispy onions
4 lime wedges
2 tsp Indonesian chile paste (*sambal oelek*) or chile sauce

● Heat the oil in a frying pan. Fry the shallots, garlic, galangal or ginger, and the ground coriander, then add the nuts. Blend to a paste with 3 tablespoons chicken stock in a mixer or food processor.

● Put the paste and chicken stock in a pan, and simmer for 5 minutes. Then add the chicken meat and salt, and simmer for 2–3 minutes. Meanwhile, soak the rice vermicelli in warm water for 3 minutes. Rinse, drain, and divide into four bowls.

● Put the bean sprouts, scallions, and celery on top of the noodles. Pour the soup in, and sprinkle with the crispy onions. Garnish with lime wedges and half a teaspoon of chile sauce to each bowl. Serve immediately.

ramen with wakame

Wakame seaweed is sold either dried or salted. The dried variety is more easily preserved and handled. *Wakame* is very nutritious, full of minerals and trace elements, and virtually calorie-free! It makes a healthy hot noodle soup dish.

1 lb *ramen* noodles, *or* 14 oz
   fresh *or* ¾ lb dried medium
   egg noodles
6 cups soy sauce broth
   (see page 26)
For the topping:
2½ tbsp dried *wakame* seaweed,
   soaked in hot water and then
   drained
4 tbsp cooked dried bamboo
   shoots (*shinachiku*) (optional)
2 scallions, chopped
2 hard-boiled eggs, cut in half

● Boil plenty of water in a pan. Add the noodles, and cook for 4 minutes. Drain, and put into four bowls.

● Heat the soy sauce broth. Place the *wakame*, bamboo shoots if used, scallions, and eggs on the noodles. Pour the soy sauce broth gently into the bowls. Serve immediately.

ramen with pork and bean curd

Pork and bean curd, called *Ma Po's Tofu* in China, is a popular family dish throughout east Asia. It is commonly served with rice. However, this spicy sauce with pork and bean curd really goes down just as well piled onto a bowl of hot noodles.

1 lb *ramen* noodles, *or* 14 oz
   fresh *or* ¾ lb dried medium
   egg noodles
6 cups soy sauce broth
   (see page 26)
2 scallions, chopped
For the topping:
1 tbsp vegetable oil
1 clove garlic, finely chopped
½-inch piece ginger, peeled and
   finely chopped
6 oz ground pork
½ leek, finely sliced
1¼ cups chicken stock
   (see page 25)
1 tbsp chile bean sauce
   (*toban djan*)
2 tsp sugar
1 tsp light soy sauce
1 tbsp Chinese rice wine or dry
   sherry
1 tsp tomato paste
14 oz bean curd (*tofu*), diced
2 tbsp cornstarch mixed with
   2 tbsp water

● To make the pork with bean curd, heat the oil in a wok or frying pan until very hot. Fry the garlic and ginger for 1 minute. Then add the pork, and stir-fry for 3–4 minutes.

● Add the leek, and stir-fry for another minute. Then add the stock, chili sauce, sugar, soy sauce, wine, and tomato paste, and bring to a boil.

● Add the bean curd, and simmer for about 5–7 minutes. Next, add the cornstarch paste, and stir to thicken.

● Boil plenty of water in a pan and add the noodles. Cook for 3 minutes, then drain. Place the noodles in individual bowls. Heat the soy broth.

● Put a quarter of the bean curd mixture and scallions onto each serving of noodles. Gently pour the broth over the top, and serve at once.

ramen with garlic

Do not be surprised at the amount of garlic used in this recipe. The key point of this dish is the strong garlic flavoring, which makes it a warming dish for a cold winter's day.

1 tbsp sesame oil
16 cloves garlic, sliced
1 lb *ramen* noodles, *or* 14 oz fresh *or* ¾ lb dried thin egg noodles
4 cloves garlic, crushed
6 cups soy sauce broth
   (see page 26)
4 tbsp cooked dried bamboo shoots (*shinachiku*) (optional)
2 scallions, chopped

● Heat the sesame oil in a frying pan. Fry the garlic for 2–3 minutes, or until turned golden brown. Set aside.
● Boil plenty of water in a pan, and add the noodles. Cook for 3 minutes, then drain. Place the noodles in individual bowls.
● Put the crushed garlic and soy sauce broth in a pan. Bring to a boil, and simmer for 2–3 minutes.
● Put a quarter of the fried garlic, bamboo shoots, and scallions onto each serving of noodles. Pour the broth over the top, and serve immediately.

ramen with stir-fried vegetables

Ramen noodles topped with a blend of fresh and flash-fried vegetables— deliciously simple and simply delicious!

1 lb *ramen* noodles, *or* 14 oz fresh *or* ¾ lb oz dried thin egg noodles
6 cups soy sauce broth
   (see page 26)
For the topping:
2 tbsp vegetable oil
1 tbsp sesame oil
1 small onion, sliced
¾ cup snowpeas, cut in half diagonally
2–3 small carrots, cut into long matchsticks
2½ cups bean sprouts
½ lb Chinese cabbage, chopped
2 dried black ear fungi or dried *shiitaki* mushrooms, soaked in water, rinsed, and chopped
salt and pepper

● Heat the oils in a wok or frying pan until very hot. Stir-fry the onion, snowpeas, and carrots for 2 minutes, then add the bean sprouts, Chinese cabbage, black fungi or mushrooms, and stir-fry for another 3–4 minutes. Season with salt and pepper.
● Boil plenty of water in a large pan, and add the noodles. Cook for 3 minutes before draining well. Put the noodles into four bowls.
● Heat the soy sauce broth. Pile the stir-fried vegetables onto the noodles, and pour the broth over the top.

Right
Ramen *with Stir-fried Vegetables*

ramen with chicken nuggets

Deep-fried, spicy chicken nuggets are a favorite in Japan, served on their own or as an accompaniment to a dish, such as below, which should fill even the emptiest stomach.

1 lb *ramen* noodles, *or* 14 oz fresh *or* ¾ lb dried thin egg noodles
6 cups soy sauce broth
 (see page 26)
4 tbsp cooked dried bamboo shoots (*shinachiku*) (optional)
watercress for garnish
For the nuggets:
black pepper
2 boneless chicken breasts, roughly diced
3 tbsp soy sauce
vegetable oil for deep frying
2 tbsp cornstarch
2 tbsp flour
½ tbsp garlic powder
½ tbsp ginger powder

● Sprinkle the black pepper over the chicken, and marinate with the soy sauce for 30 minutes. Heat the oil to 350°F in a saucepan. Mix the cornstarch, flour, garlic powder, and ginger powder together in a bowl. Coat the chicken with the flour mixture, and deep fry until golden brown.

● Boil plenty of water in a pan, and boil the noodles for 3 minutes or according to the package instructions. Drain and put into four bowls.

● Heat the soy sauce broth. Place the chicken nuggets, bamboo shoots, and watercress on the noodles, then pour the broth over the top.

ramen with barbecued pork

cha siu mein

Cha siu is a spicy Chinese marinade, and *cha siu* pork is widely eaten all over southeast Asia. *Cha siu* pork is roasted for a comparatively short time compared to roast pork dishes prepared in the West, leaving the inner part of the meat nearly rare. *Cha siu* sauce is available from Chinese stores and larger supermarkets.

1 lb *ramen* noodles, *or* 14 oz fresh *or* ¾ lb dried thin egg noodles
6 cups soy sauce broth *(see page 26)*
For the topping:
12 large slices Chinese style barbecued pork (*cha siu*)
4 tbsp cooked dried bamboo shoots (*shinachiku*) (optional)
3 scallions, chopped

● Boil plenty of water in a pan, and cook the noodles for 3 minutes. Drain and divide into four bowls. Heat the soy sauce broth.

● Put three slices of *cha siu* into each bowl of noodles. Garnish with the bamboo shoots and scallions. Pour the soy sauce broth over the top just before serving.

How to make *cha siu* pork

2 lb pork tenderloin
8 tbsp *cha siu* sauce for marinating

Marinate the pork in the *cha siu* sauce for at least an hour but preferably 3–4 hours. Preheat the oven to 375°F. Place the pork on a rack on a baking tray lined with aluminum foil. Bake for 60–70 minutes, basting a few times. The outside of the pork should be browned and the inside still tender.

Right
Ramen *with Barbecued Pork*

ramen with crab omelet

kanitama-ramen

Typically, crab omelet is served on its own. The inspiration behind the dish is Chinese, but the Japanese have a preference for it served on a bowl of noodles. Ideally, individual omelets should be made, but if time is against you, make one large one and cut it into four portions.

1 lb *ramen* noodles, *or* 14 oz fresh *or* ¾ lb dried thin egg noodles
6 cups soy sauce broth *(see page 26)*

For the omelet:
6 eggs
6 oz crabmeat (canned)
4 *shiitake* mushrooms, sliced
2 scallions, thinly sliced
4 tbsp canned bamboo shoots, thinly sliced
salt and white pepper
2–3 tbsp vegetable oil
1 scallion, chopped

● First, to make the omelet, put the eggs, crabmeat, mushrooms, scallion, and bamboo shoots in a bowl. Season with salt and pepper, and mix.
● Heat the oil in a frying pan or wok until very hot. Pour in the egg mixture, and heat for 30 seconds. Stir lightly with chopsticks or a spatula a few times. When it is nearly set, turn it over. The mixture should be soft like scrambled eggs, but be cooked just enough to be able to retain the shape of an omelet.
● Boil plenty of water in a large pan. Add the noodles and cook for 3 minutes, or according to the instructions on the package. Drain, then divide into four bowls.

● Heat the soy sauce broth. Place the crab omelet on the noodles, and pour the broth over the top. Sprinkle with the chopped scallion and serve.

ramen with wontons

Wontons, spicy parcels of ground pork, are another Chinese creation that has been exported far and wide. Wonton wrappers are available from oriental food stores, and can be frozen. Slippery little creatures that they are, wonton parcels served in a bowl of noodles demand good chopstick technique if a humiliating resort to a spoon is to be avoided!

¾ lb *ramen* or fresh thin egg noodles
6 cups soy sauce broth *(see page 26)*
2 large lettuce leaves, blanched
3 scallions, chopped

For the wontons:
scant ¼ lb ground pork
1 scallion, finely chopped
1 dried *shiitake* mushroom, soaked in hot water, then finely chopped
¼-inch piece fresh ginger, peeled and sliced
½ tsp light soy sauce
¼ tsp Chinese rice wine or dry sherry
¼ tsp sesame oil
salt
20 wonton wrappers

● Mix the ground pork, scallion, *shiitake* mushroom, ginger, soy sauce, rice wine, sesame oil, and salt together

in a bowl. Take 1 teaspoon of the meat mixture and put it on the center of a wonton wrapper. Wet the edge with water, and fold over into a clam shape. Seal the edge well, taking care to press out any air caught inside the wonton. Next draw the two ends, wet one side with water, and pinch together. Make the rest of the wontons in the same way.
● Bring water in two saucepans to a boil. Cook the noodles for 3 minutes in one of them, and boil the wontons for about 3–4 minutes in the other saucepan. Drain the noodles and wontons well. First, divide the noodles into four bowls, then put the wontons on top of the noodles.
● Heat the soy sauce broth. Place the blanched lettuce and scallion on the noodles. Pour the broth over the top, then serve at once.

Right
Ramen *with Crab Omelet.*

Above
Ramen
with Corn
and Butter.

shoyu-ramen

This dish is beginning to be popular in the west as a lunch dish or light meal, while melted butter and corn are particular Japanese favorites.

I lb *ramen* noodles
6 cups chicken stock
  (see *page 25*)
6 tbsp Japanese soy sauce
I tsp salt
a pinch of freshly ground black
  pepper
For the topping:
I cup canned corn kernels
6 scallions, chopped
3 tbsp butter sliced into four

● Boil the noodles for about 2–2½ minutes. Drain, and put them in individual bowls.

● Heat the stock, soy sauce, salt, and pepper in a pan. When it boils, pour the soup into the bowls. Put ¼ cup of the corn on top of the noodles, sprinkle with the chopped scallions, then top with the butter. Eat as soon as possible or the noodles will absorb the stock and become soggy.

miso ramen with corn

The *miso* broth used in this dish has a sweet, spicy flavor. The taste of the broth will differ depending on the variety of *miso* used. Once you have prepared the tasty broth, this simple and quick *ramen* dish is ready to eat in minutes. For an easy variation, try a pat of butter dropped onto the noodles to enrich the taste.

I lb *ramen* noodles, *or* 14 oz
  fresh *or* ¾ lb dried thin egg
  noodles
6 cups *miso* broth (see *page 25*)
For the topping:
I cup canned corn
handful alfalfa sprouts
3 scallions, chopped
½ sheet *nori* seaweed, cut in
  four

● Boil plenty of water in a pan. Add the noodles, and cook for 3 minutes. Drain, and divide into individual bowls.

● Heat the *miso* broth. Pile the corn onto the noodles, then add the sprouts, scallions, and *nori*. Gently pour the *miso* broth over the top, and serve at once.

miso ramen with bean sprouts

In this recipe, medium egg noodles are used. but thin egg noodles can be used in their place if wished. When you blanch the bean sprouts, take care not to overcook them. They should still be crispy when eaten.

5 cups bean sprouts
I lb *ramen* noodles, *or* 14 oz
  fresh *or* ¾ lb dried thin egg
  noodles
6 cups *miso* broth (see *page 25*)
½ sheet *nori* seaweed, cut into
  four
alfalfa sprouts to garnish

● Boil water in a pan, and blanch the bean sprouts for 30 seconds. Drain.

● Boil plenty of water in a pan, and add the noodles. Cook for 3 minutes, then drain. Place the noodles in individual bowls.

● Heat the *miso* broth. Put a quarter of the bean sprouts, a square of *nori*, and some sprouts onto each serving of noodles, and pour the *miso* broth over the top. Serve immediately.

Right
Miso
Ramen
with Corn

Above

Noodles
with a
Jumbo
Shrimp

noodles with a jumbo shrimp

Topping a dish of *soba* noodles with a jumbo shrimp turns a nourishing meal into a gourmet experience.

4 jumbo shrimp
a little flour
8 shiitake mushrooms
14 oz dried *soba*
For the batter:
4 tbsp flour
1 egg, beaten
½ cup water
6 cups *dashi* (see page 26)

● To make the topping, mix the flour, egg, and water lightly in a bowl. Coat the shrimp with flour, then dip in the batter. Dip the mushrooms into the batter as well. Heat the oil to 350°F, and deep fry until golden brown.

● Bring a large pan of water to a boil. Add the *soba,* and cook for about 5 minutes. Briefly rinse with cold water, then drain. Divide the *soba* equally between four bowls.

● Bring the Dashi Broth to a boil in a saucepan. Add to the bowls of *soba.*

● Place one shrimp and two mushrooms on the top of each bowl. Serve immediately.

miso ramen with shredded leek

Noodles in *miso* broth are one of the most popular noodle dishes served in Japan. It is essential to use a good quality *miso* paste as this provides the crucial sweet and salty flavoring to the dish. The shredded leek should have a firm, supple texture, so if prepared beforehand, soak it in a little water to prevent it from drying out.

½ lb fresh spinach
1 lb *ramen* noodles, or 14 oz
**   fresh or ¾ lb dried egg noodles**
6 cups *miso* broth (see page 25)
4-inch piece of leek, cut in four
**   pieces and shredded**
4 tbsp cooked dried bamboo
**   shoots (*shinachiku*) (optional)**

● Bring some water to a boil in a pan, and blanch the spinach for 1–2 minutes. Rinse, drain, and divide into four equal portions.

● Bring more water to a boil in a large saucepan. Add the noodles, and boil for 4 minutes. Drain, and place into individual serving bowls.

● Heat the *miso* broth for 2–3 minutes. Pile the leek, spinach, and bamboo shoots on top of the noodles. Add the *miso* broth, and serve immediately.

Right
Miso
Ramen
with
Shredded
Leek

egg noodle soup with pork chop

You would be hard pressed to find a better way of serving pork chops than with the fiery, sweet marinade used here. Strictly speaking, Chinese rice wine should be used in this dish, but I have found that a dry sherry can be used as a substitute without any drastic change in flavor.

4 pork chops off the bone, lightly tenderized

6 cups chicken stock (*see page 25*)

1 tbsp Chinese rice wine or dry sherry

2 tsp salt

white pepper

2 lettuce leaves, quartered

4–5 tbsp vegetable oil

1 lb *ramen* **noodles,** *or* **14 oz fresh** *or* **¾ lb dried medium egg noodles**

For the marinade:

1 clove garlic, finely chopped

1 scallion, chopped

1 tbsp light soy sauce

1 tbsp dark soy sauce

2 tbsp Chinese rice wine or dry sherry

1 tbsp sugar

a pinch of pepper

2 tsp cornstarch

● Mix the garlic, scallion, soy sauce, rice wine, sugar, pepper, and cornstarch together, then marinate the pork chops for 30 minutes.

● Meanwhile, put the chicken stock, rice wine, salt, and pepper in a pan. Bring to a boil, and simmer for 3 minutes. Blanch the lettuce leaves in a pan for 1 minute. Set aside.

● Heat the oil in a wok or frying pan. Shallow fry the pork chops for 2–3 minutes on each side until lightly browned. (Frying time will vary with the thickness of the pork.) Cut into 1-inch strips.

● Bring plenty of water to a boil in a large pan, and add the egg noodles. Cook for 4 minutes, or according to the instructions on the package. Drain well, and put into four bowls.

● Place the pork and lettuce leaves on the noodles, and pour the hot broth over the top. Serve immediately.

udon noodles with egg

kakitama-udon

Udon is a great favorite in the winter months because of its warming properties. *Udon* comes in various shapes, some flat, some round in section, some as thick as a little finger, others as thin as spaghetti.

1¼ lb parboiled fresh *udon*
  (see page 24)
For the soup:
6 cups *dashi broth* (see page 26)
2 eggs, beaten
4 tsp cornstarch
4 tsp water
4 scallions, chopped

● Bring a large pan of water to a boil. Add the *udon*, and boil for 2 minutes. Drain, and then place in equal portions into the four bowls.

● Put the *dashi* broth in a saucepan, and bring to a boil. Pour two-thirds of the liquid into the four bowls. Bring the remainder back to a boil and gradually add the egg, mixing lightly so that when the egg rises to the surface, it is cooked in fronds.

● Mix the cornstarch and water into a paste, and then add this to the soup to thicken. Pour the egg mixture into the bowls. Sprinkle with the scallions, and serve immediately.

egg noodle soup with spicy sesame sauce

dan dan mian

This is a famous Sichuan dish, although it has gained popularity in other Asian countries. There are several versions to this recipe, but all include the rich aromatic sesame sauce, which gives full flavor to the soup. You can adjust the amount of chile oil to your liking.

1 lb *ramen* noodles, or 14 oz
  fresh *or* ¾ lb dried thin egg
  noodles
5½ cups chicken stock
  (see page 25)
For the spicy sesame sauce:
1 tbsp vegetable oil
1-inch piece fresh ginger, peeled
  and finely chopped
3 cloves garlic, finely chopped
½ lb ground pork
8 *shiitake* mushrooms, finely
  chopped
4 scallions, finely chopped
6 tbsp sesame sauce
5 tbsp light soy sauce
1 tbsp chile oil

● First, to make the spicy sesame sauce, heat the oil in a frying pan. Fry the ginger and garlic for 30 seconds, add the pork, mushrooms, and scallions, then stir-fry for 3–4 minutes.

● Add the sesame sauce, soy sauce, chile oil, and stir for 1–2 minutes. Set aside.

● Boil plenty of water in a pan, add the noodles, and cook for about 3 minutes or according to the instructions on the package. Drain and divide into four bowls.

● Heat the chicken stock. Pour the spicy sesame sauce over the noodles. Gently pour the stock into the bowls. Serve at once.

sukiyaki udon

Sukiyaki itself is a famous Japanese dish. *Udon* are often combined with *sukiyaki* in Japanese homes, stirred in alongside the steak and vegetables and left to cook and absorb all the delicious flavors cooking away in the pot.

⅔ cup premier *dashi* (*see page 26*)
1½ tbsp sugar
2 tbsp Japanese rice wine (*sake*)
2½ tbsp soy sauce
2 scallions, chopped
½ lb rump steak, thinly sliced in 2-inch strips
½ leek, sliced diagonally
4 leaves of Chinese cabbage, diced
4 *shiitake* mushrooms, halved
1¼ lb parboiled fresh *udon*
6 cups *dashi* broth (*see page 26*)

To make the sukiyaki:
● Put the *dashi*, sugar, sake, and soy sauce into a pan and bring to a boil. Add the steak, leek, Chinese cabbage leaves, and *shiitake*, then simmer for 7–10 minutes. Set aside.
● Boil plenty of water in a pan. Add the *udon*, and boil for 3 minutes. Drain, and rinse with cold water. Drain again, and divide into four bowls.
● Heat the broth. Place the sukiyaki on top of the noodles, and pour the broth over the top. Serve immediately.

udon with bean curd sheet
kitsune udon

Abura-age are deep-fried sheets of *tofu*, available at most stores that stock Japanese foodstuffs. They can be stored at home in the freezer, but will quickly spoil if left for any time in the refrigerator.

1¼ lb parboiled fresh *udon*
6 cups *dashi* broth (*see page 26*)
For the topping:
4 bean curd sheets (*abura-age*), cut into halves
1 cup premier *dashi* (*see page 26*)
2 tbsp sugar
2½ tbsp soy sauce
½ lb fresh spinach
2 scallions, chopped
a pinch of salt
seven flavors chile powder (*shichimi*) (optional)

● Rinse the *abura-age* in hot water. Put it into a saucepan of boiling water, together with the *dashi*, sugar, and soy sauce. Simmer for about 20 minutes, or until the fluid has reduced to a third.
● Bring plenty of water to boil in a pan, and add the *udon*. Cook for 3 minutes. Drain and rinse with cold water, then drain once more. Divide into individual serving bowls.
● Blanch the spinach in boiling water for 1 minute, then drain and squeeze out the excess water. Heat the *dashi* broth.
● Put two half-sheets of *abura-age*, some spinach, and scallions onto each serving of *udon*. Pour the broth over the top, sprinkle with the seven flavors chile powder, and serve.

udon with egg strands

tamago-toji udon

The addition of beaten egg to a bowl of *udon* enriches the noodles and thickens the broth while retaining the essential lightness of the dish. The strands of egg are easy to make as long as the beaten egg is dribbled into the broth, not added all at once. For the best result, do as I have done here, and beat the strands into individual portions of broth.

1¼ lb parboiled fresh *udon*
6 cups *dashi* broth (see page 26)
3 eggs, beaten
watercress for garnish

● Bring plenty of water to boil in a pan, and add the *udon*. Cook for 3 minutes. Drain, and rinse with cold water. Drain once more. Divide and place in individual serving bowls.
● Bring the *dashi* broth to a boil, and pour one quarter into a saucepan. To make the "egg flowers," dribble a quarter of the beaten egg into the saucepan, stirring occasionally with a chopstick or similar to pull out the strands. Repeat three more times. Pour the egg strand broth onto the noodles, garnish with the watercress, and serve immediately.

udon with five toppings

okame udon

A filling dish of *udon* with several toppings. To make the Japanese-style omelet successfully, a non-stick pan is essential. If you can't find a shop that stocks Japanese fish cake, or *kamaboko*, imitation crabmeat can be pressed into service in its place.

1¼ lb parboiled fresh *udon*
6 cups *dashi* broth (see page 26)
For the topping
4 *shiitake* mushrooms
1⅓ cups *dashi* (see page 26)
2½ tbsp soy sauce
2½ tbsp *mirin*
½ lb fresh spinach
4 slices Japanese fish cake (*kamaboko*) or imitation crabmeat
generous handful alfalfa sprouts
For the omelets:
2 eggs
2 tsp *mirin*
¼ tsp soy sauce
a pinch of salt
2 tsp vegetable oil

● Put the *shiitake*, *dashi*, soy sauce, and *mirin* into a saucepan, bring to a boil, and simmer for 8–10 minutes before setting aside. Discard the liquid when the *shiitake* are ready to be added to the *udon*.
● To make the egg omelet, beat the eggs, *mirin*, soy sauce, and salt together in a bowl. Heat the oil in a frying pan. Pour a third of the egg mixture into the pan. When it is half set, gently roll it up and over to one side of the pan. Add another third of the mixture. Wait until this has half set, roll the first third over to the other side of the pan so it picks up the second third as it

goes. Repeat once more before leaving to cool. When cooled, cut into eight pieces.
● Cook the spinach in boiling water for 1–2 minutes. Rinse with cold water, and squeeze out thoroughly. Cut into four portions.
● Cook the *udon* in a saucepan of boiling water for about 3 minutes. Rinse, drain, and divide equally into four bowls.
● Heat the *dashi* broth. Put one *shiitake* mushroom, 2 slices of omelet, 1 portion of spinach, 1 slice of fish cake, and a quarter of the sprouts into each bowl. Pour the hot *dashi* broth over the top, and serve immediately.

Left
Udon *with*
Five
Toppings

kishimen udon

Kishimen is a flat Japanese variation on *udon*, not unlike Chinese rick-stick noodles, or Italian fettucine if you prefer a European analogy. The recipe below pairs them with a light and nutritious combination of fresh vegetables and seafood.

1¼ lb parboiled fresh *kishimen*
  or *udon*
6 cups *dashi* broth *(see page 26)*
For the topping:
8 snowpeas
8 pieces imitation crabmeat
½ sheet *nori* seaweed, cut into
  four strips
4 scallions, chopped

● Cook the snowpeas in a pan of boiling water for 2 minutes. Rinse with cold water, and set aside.

● Bring plenty of water to a boil in a saucepan, and add the noodles. Boil for 3 minutes, then drain and rinse with cold water. Drain again, and then divide into four serving bowls.

● Place 2 snowpeas, 2 pieces imitation crabmeat, I strip of *nori*, and a quarter of the scallions on top of each serving. Heat the *dashi* broth and pour into the bowls. Serve immediately.

udon with pork
butaniku iri udon

A deceptively simple, wholesome dish with its origin in the Japanese peasantry. You might find it hard to believe that something so simple to prepare could taste so good.

6 cups *dashi* broth *(see page 26)*
½ lb lean pork, thinly sliced on a
  slant into bite-sized pieces
I leek, sliced diagonally
I packet *shimeji* (or *shiitake*)
  mushrooms
1¼ lb parboiled fresh *udon*
2 eggs, beaten
2 scallions, chopped
seven flavor chile powder
  (shichimi) (optional)

● Bring the broth to a boil in a pan, then add the pork, leek, and mushrooms, and simmer for about 5 minutes until the leek has softened.

● Add the *udon*, and simmer for 3 minutes. When the broth comes to a boil, pour in the beaten egg and wait for it to firm. Pile the mixture into bowls, sprinkle with the *shichimi*, and serve immediately.

udon with curry sauce

kare udon

A modern Japanese innovation combining the spicy flavor of a curry sauce, with the smooth texture of *udon* noodles.

1¼ lb parboiled fresh **udon**
6 cups *dashi* broth *(see page 26)*
For the curry:
2 tbsp vegetable oil
2 boneless chicken breasts, diced
1 medium-sized onion, sliced
2 tbsp flour
1–2 tsp curry powder
½ chicken stock cube
1½ cups water
2 tbsp chutney
⅓ cup raisins
salt and pepper

● Heat the oil in a pan. Fry the chicken for 5 minutes, or until cooked through. Set aside.
● Add the onion, and fry until lightly browned. Add the flour and curry powder, and fry for 1–2 minutes.
● Gradually dissolve the chicken stock into the water, add the chutney and raisins, and season with salt and pepper. Simmer for 10 minutes, then stir in the cooked chicken.
● Bring plenty of water to a boil in a pan, and add the *udon*. Cook for 3 minutes, and drain. Rinse under cold water, and drain again. Divide into serving bowls.
● Meanwhile, heat the broth. Pour the curry sauce over the *udon*, and pour the broth over the top. Serve immediately.

Right
Udon *with*
Curry
Sauce

wakame udon

This tasty and filling dish is full of sea-sourced protein and minerals derived from *wakame* seaweed and Japanese fish cake.

1¼ lb parboiled fresh *udon*
6 cups *dashi* broth (*see page 26*)
For the topping:
4 tbsp bamboo shoots (canned)
⅔ cup premier *dashi* (*see page 26*)
1 tbsp soy sauce
1 tbsp *mirin*
4 tsp dried *wakame* seaweed
8 slices Japanese fish cake (*kamaboko*), or imitation crabmeat
3 scallions, chopped
seven flavor chile powder (*shichimi*) (optional)

● Put the bamboo shoots, *dashi*, soy sauce, and *mirin* into a pan, and simmer for 7–10 minutes. Set aside.
● Bring plenty of water to a boil in a pan, and add the *udon*. Cook for 3 minutes, and drain. Rinse with cold water, and drain again. Divide equally into four bowls.
● Heat the *dashi* broth. Put a quarter of the bamboo shoots, 1 teaspoon *wakame*, 2 slices of fish cake, and a quarter of the scallions into each bowl. Pour the hot broth over the top, sprinkle with *shichimi,* and serve immediately.

udon stew

nabe-yaki udon

This dish is ideally prepared in individual clay pots and served straight from the stove but you can use a large stew pot or pan with a lid and divide into four serving bowls.

vegetable oil for deep frying
5 tbsp flour
½ egg, beaten
½ cup cold water
4 jumbo shrimp, peeled
7 cups *dashi* broth (*see page 26*)
1¼ lb parboiled fresh *udon*
8 *shiitake* mushrooms
1 package *enoki* mushrooms, or 8 button mushrooms
½ leek, sliced diagonally
8 snowpeas
4 scallions
4 eggs

● Fill a pan one-third full of oil, and heat to 350°F. Mix 4 tablespoons of the flour, the beaten egg, and water lightly in a bowl to make the batter. Dust the shrimp with the remaining flour, and dip into the batter. Deep-fry in the oil until golden and crisp. Set aside.
● Heat the *dashi* broth in a pan. Add the *udon* and place the mushrooms, leek, snowpeas, and scallions on top. Cover, and cook for 3 minutes. Add the shrimp, then crack the eggs into the broth, taking care not to break the yolks; cover, and simmer.
● When the surface of the eggs turn white, the dish is ready to serve.

miso udon stew

If you use dried *udon,* boil it *al dente* first. You can skip the chicken and make vegetarian hot pot, if you wish. *Gobo,* a fibrous root vegetable, is available from Japanese grocers.

7½ cups premier *dashi* (*see page 26*)
½ lb boneless chicken breasts, diced
3 small carrots, sliced
6 oz rutabaga, sliced into bite-sized pieces
½ leek, sliced diagonally
2 tbsp Japanese rice wine (*sake*)
2 oz *shimeji* mushrooms or 8 *shiitake* mushrooms
1 oz *gobo* (optional), thinly sliced
1¼ lb parboiled fresh *udon,* rinsed
8 tbsp *miso* paste

● Put the *dashi,* chicken, carrots, rutabaga, and leek in a saucepan, bring to a boil, and then add the *sake,* mushrooms, and *gobo* (if using). Simmer for 10–12 minutes.
● Add the *udon,* and cook for 3 minutes. Stir in the *miso* paste. When it comes back to a boil, it is ready to serve.

Right
Miso Udon
Stew

udon vegetable stew

kenchin udon

Kenchin jiru is a vegetable stew, originally prepared for Buddhist monks. It is a very simple and delicate dish as only vegetables are used, but it will without doubt warm you up on a cold winter's day. This recipe includes several vegetables that may be unfamiliar: they are described in the glossary, and are available from Japanese grocers.

2 tbsp sesame oil
6 oz carrots, cut at random into bite-sized pieces
6 oz *mooli* (*daikon*), quartered and sliced
10 oz *satoimo* or new potatoes, diced
1 oz *gobo* (optional), thinly sliced diagonally
6 oz bean curd (*tofu*), diced
7½ cups premier *dashi* (*see page 26*)
2 tbsp Japanese rice wine (*sake*)
2 tsp sugar
2 tsp salt
3 tbsp Japanese soy sauce
1¼ lb parboiled fresh *udon*, rinsed
3 scallions, chopped

● Heat the sesame oil in a saucepan. Stir-fry the carrots, *mooli, satoimo,* and *gobo* for 2 minutes. Then add the bean curd and stir.
● Add the *dashi* and *sake,* and bring to a boil. Add the sugar, salt, and soy sauce, and simmer for 8–10 minutes.
● Add the *udon* and scallions, and simmer for a further 3 minutes. Serve immediately.

soba with egg

tsukimi soba

This dish draws its name from the egg yolk that tops it off and is said to resemble the full moon (*tsukimi* means "moon-watching" in Japanese).

14 oz dried *soba*
6 cups *dashi* broth (*see page 26*)
4 egg yolks
2 sheets of *nori* seaweed, shredded
alfalfa sprouts to garnish

● Bring plenty of water to a boil in a large pan, and add the *soba.* Cook for 5–6 minutes. Drain, and rinse well under cold water. Drain again. Divide into individual bowls.
● Bring the *dashi* broth to a boil, and pour into each bowl.
● Place an egg yolk in the center of each bowl, and sprinkle the *nori* and sprouts around the egg. Serve immediately.

soba with grated yam

yamakake soba

The *yama-imo* or mountain potato is a Japanese member of the yam family. *Yama-imo* can be eaten as here, grated into a thick, spongy topping. Japanese *yama-imo,* which tends not to discolor so quickly when peeled, is recommended for this dish.

14 oz dried *soba*
6 cups *dashi* broth (*see page 26*)
For the topping:
¾ lb yam (*yama-imo*)
4 quails eggs
1 sheet of *nori* seaweed, shredded
3 scallions, chopped
2 tsp *wasabi* mustard (optional)

● Heat the *dashi* broth.
● Bring plenty of water to a boil in a large pan, and add the *soba.* Cook for 5–6 minutes. Drain, and rinse well under cold water. Drain again. Divide into serving bowls.
● Peel the yam little by little as you grate it to stop it from slipping out of your fingers.
● Put the grated yam over the *soba,* then break the eggs into the center of the grated yam. Sprinkle with *nori* and scallions. Put a ½ teaspoon of *wasabi* at the edge of each bowl.
● Gently pour the *dashi* over the top, and serve immediately.

Right
Soba *with Grated Yam*

soba with batter

tanuki soba

This dish is usually named because the *tanuki*, or badger, is reputed to have a fondness for the small droplets of batter used to top the noodles. The batter is the same type as used to make *tempura*, so any leftovers can be gainfully put to use.

14 oz dried *soba*
6 cups *dashi* broth (*see page 26*)
For the topping:
vegetable oil for frying
4 tbsp flour
½ a beaten egg
generous ½ cup water
8 snowpeas
3 scallions, chopped

● Bring plenty of water to a boil in a large pan, and add the *soba*. Cook for 5–6 minutes. Drain, and rinse well under cold water. Drain again. Divide into serving bowls.
● To make the topping, heat the oil to 350°F in a pan. Mix the flour, egg, and water lightly in a bowl. Using chopsticks, drip the mixture into the oil a little at a time, trying to avoid making big lumps of batter. When the batter has turned golden brown and floats to the surface, it is ready. Drain on paper towels.
● Meanwhile, blanch the snowpeas for 2 minutes, rinse with cold water, and then drain.
● Heat the *dashi* broth.
● Place 2 tablespoonfuls of the batter in the center of each bowl, on top of the noodles. Place 2 snowpeas on top, and sprinkle with the chopped scallion. Pour the *dashi* broth in gently, and serve immediately.

soba with three mushrooms

The Japanese have a great fondness for mushrooms. This dish combines three varieties, each with its own particular shape, texture, and flavor. If *shimeji* or *enoki* mushrooms are unavailable, ordinary button mushrooms or oyster mushrooms can be used instead.

14 oz dried *soba*
6 cups *dashi* broth (*see page 26*)
For the topping:
1½ cups *premier dashi*
  (*see page 26*)
1 tbsp *mirin*
2 tbsp soy sauce
1 tbsp sugar
8 *shiitake* mushrooms
¼ lb fresh *shimeji* mushrooms,
  the bottom of the roots
  cut off
½ lb fresh *enoki* mushrooms, the
  bottom of the roots cut off
½ lb fresh spinach

● Put the *dashi*, *mirin*, soy sauce, and sugar in a saucepan. Bring to a boil, then add the *shiitake* and *shimeji* mushrooms and simmer for 4–5 minutes. Add the *enoki* mushrooms, and simmer for a further 2–3 minutes.
● Blanch the spinach in boiling water for 1–2 minutes. Rinse under water and squeeze out any excess water. Boil plenty of water in a pan and cook the *soba* for 5–6 minutes, or according to the instruction on the package. Rinse under water, drain, and then divide into four bowls.
● Heat the *dashi* broth. Arrange the mushrooms and spinach on the *soba*. Pour the *dashi* broth over the top, and serve immediately.

soba with chicken

tori-nanban

The chicken used in this dish should be marinated for as long as possible to extract as much flavor from the sauce as possible, so don't be tempted to cut down on the times below, which should be treated as a minimum.

14 oz dried *soba*
6 cups *dashi* broth (*see page 26*)
For the topping:
3 boneless chicken breasts,
  sliced on a slant into bite-
  sized pieces
2 tbsp Japanese soy sauce
1 leek, thinly sliced diagonally
seven flavors chile powder
  (*shichimi*) (optional)
alfalfa sprouts for garnish

● Marinate the chicken in the soy sauce for at least 15 minutes. Put the chicken, leek, and *dashi* broth in a saucepan, bring to a boil, and simmer for 10–15 minutes, or until the chicken is cooked. Occasionally skim off the scum which will form on top.
● Boil plenty of water in a large pan, and add the soba. Cook for 5–6 minutes. Rinse well under water, and drain thoroughly. Divide the *soba* into four bowls.
● Pour the broth with chicken and leek into the bowls. Garnish with the sprouts. Sprinkle with *shichimi*, and then serve at once.

Right
Soba *with*
Chicken

soba with simmered herring

nishin soba

In Japan, this dish requires the use of a kind of smoked herring not usually available overseas. For this recipe, I have found that kippers make an excellent substitute.

14 oz dried *soba*
6 cups *dashi* broth *(see page 26)*
For the topping:
4 kipper fillets
2 tbsp soy sauce
2 tbsp *mirin*
2 tbsp sugar
½ cup water
3 scallions, chopped
seven flavor chile powder
   (*shichimi*) (optional)

● Rinse the kippers in hot water. Put them, together with the soy sauce, *mirin*, sugar, and water, into a pan and simmer for about 20 minutes, or until the sauce has thickened.
● Bring plenty of water to boil in a pan, and add the *soba*. Cook for 5–6 minutes. Drain, and rinse well under cold water. Drain again. Divide into serving bowls.
● Heat the *dashi* broth.
● Place a kipper fillet onto each serving of *soba,* and sprinkle with chopped scallion. Pour the broth over the top, sprinkle with *shichimi,* and serve immediately.

soba with deep-fried jumbo shrimp

tempura soba

A dish of contrasts: the light, subtle taste of the dashi broth set against the richness of the deep-fried shrimp. Expensive as they are, try to get shrimp of a decent size as they will shrink during cooking.

14 oz dried *soba*
6 cups *dashi* broth *(see page 26)*
For the topping:
vegetable oil for deep frying
8 jumbo shrimp with tails,
   peeled
½ cup plus 1 tbsp flour
1 egg, beaten
1 cup cold water
2 scallions, chopped
seven flavors chile powder
   (*shichimi*), (optional)

● Fill a pan one-third full with the oil, and heat to 350°F. Lightly mix ½ cup of the flour with the egg and water. Coat the shrimp with the remaining flour, then dip into the batter. Deep fry until golden brown. Drain on paper towels.
● Boil plenty of water in a pan, and add the *soba*. Cook for 5–6 minutes. Rinse with water, and drain. Divide into four bowls.
● Heat the *dashi* broth. Place two shrimp on each serving of *soba,* and sprinkle with scallions. Pour the *dashi* broth over the top, sprinkle with *shichimi,* and serve at once.

Right
Soba *with*
Simmered
Herring

cold noodle dishes

N *oodles are even eaten on humid summer days in southeast Asia, when bowls of noodles are converted into cold dishes. Simple, cold soba and somen dishes are very popular and low in calories. Egg noodles served in a tasty sauce are irresistable, and there are some delicious noodle salads.*

chilled egg noodles with tuna, shrimp, wakame, and sesame sauce

Noodles are just as delicious served cold as they are hot. Because they still tend to dry quickly, it is important to eat them as soon as they have been prepared and cooled.

1 lb fresh thin egg noodles
2 tsp sesame oil
For the dressing:
4 tbsp sesame sauce
4 tbsp sugar
4 tbsp vinegar
4 tbsp Japanese soy sauce
4 tbsp chicken stock (see page 25)
½-inch piece fresh ginger
For the topping:
4 tsp dried *wakame* seaweed, soaked in hot water, then drained
8 oz tuna (in water)
½ cup canned corn
8 tbsp cooked shrimp
generous handful alfalfa sprouts

● Bring a large pan of water to a boil. Cook the noodles for 3 minutes, then rinse and drain. Toss the noodles in the sesame oil, then place onto four serving plates.
● Mix the sesame sauce, sugar, vinegar, soy sauce, and chicken stock well. Extract the juice from the ginger by grating it then squeezing out the juice by hand. Add it to the mixture, and mix again. Refrigerate.
● Divide the seaweed, tuna, corn, shrimp, and sprouts among each serving of the noodles.
● Pour the sesame dressing over each serving, and serve immediately.

chilled egg noodles with chicken and pepper salami

Pepper salami is not an authentic topping, but it really goes well with chilled noodles.

1 lb fresh or ¾ lb dried thin egg noodles
1 tbsp sesame oil
For the sauce:
generous 1 cup chicken stock (see page 25)
½ cup light soy sauce
4 tbsp sugar
½ cup vinegar
4 tsp sesame oil
2 tbsp squeezed ginger juice
For the topping:
2 boneless chicken breasts
2 eggs, beaten
2 tsp sugar
1 tbsp vegetable oil
5-inch piece cucumber, thinly sliced diagonally and cut into long matchsticks
8 slices pepper salami, cut into long matchsticks
4 tsp red pickled ginger (beni-shouga) (optional)
4 tsp toasted sesame seeds

● Boil plenty of water in a pan, and add the noodles. Cook for 3 minutes, and rinse with cold water. Drain, then toss the noodles in 1 tablespoon sesame oil. Arrange on four shallow dishes.
● To prepare the sauce, heat the stock, soy sauce, and sugar in a pan, and simmer for 3 minutes. Turn off the heat and add the vinegar, 4 teaspoons sesame oil, and the ginger juice. Mix well before refrigerating

● Boil the chicken in a pan for about 15–20 minutes. Let it cool, then pull into shreds with your fingers or a knife. Set aside. Keep the water in the pan as stock for another use.
● Mix the beaten egg and sugar together in a bowl. Heat 1 teaspoon of oil in an omelet pan, and pour a third of the egg mixture into it. When the egg is half set, turn it over. Repeat this to make two more thin omelets, using fresh oil each time. When the omelets are cooled, cut them in half and shred.
● Arrange the chicken, egg, cucumber, and pepper salami on the noodles. Put the red pickled ginger (if using) on top, and sprinkle with the sesame seeds. Pour the chilled sauce over prior to eating.

toasted sesame seeds

This is simple to do. Just roast the sesame seeds in a frying pan without any oil. When the sesame seeds puff up and you can smell their aromatic flavor, they are ready. It is a good idea to roast a large amount of seeds, and then keep them in a jar for future use.

Right
Chilled Egg Noodles with Tuna, Shrimp, Wakame, and Sesame Sauce

chilled egg noodles with mackerel and shrimp

This recipe is just perfect for one of those summer's days when you are hungry but can't face the thought of eating anything hot.

1 lb fresh or ¾ lb dried thin egg noodles
For the sauce:
generous 1 cup chicken stock (see page 25)
½ cup light soy sauce
4 tbsp sugar
½ cup vinegar
4 tsp sesame oil
2 tbsp juice of squeezed ginger
For the topping:
1½ cups bean sprouts
¼ lb snowpeas
1 large fillet smoked mackerel, flaked
¼ lb cooked shrimp
handful alfalfa sprouts
1 medium-sized tomato, sliced

● Boil plenty of water in a pan, add the noodles, and cook for 3 minutes. Rinse under water, drain, and arrange on four shallow dishes.
● Heat the chicken stock, soy sauce, and sugar in a pan, and simmer for 3 minutes. Add the vinegar, sesame oil, and ginger juice, and mix well. Chill in the refrigerator.
● Blanch the bean sprouts and snowpeas for 1 minute in boiling water. Remove and cut the snowpeas into long matchsticks. Now arrange the mackerel flakes, shrimp, bean sprouts, snowpeas, alfalfa sprouts, and tomato on the noodles. Pour the chilled sauce over and serve at once.

chilled egg noodles with chicken and peanut sauce

A well-loved Chinese noodle dish. It can be prepared with any type of peanut butter, depending on your preference for smooth or crunchy.

1 lb boneless chicken breasts
1 lb fresh thin egg noodles
2 tsp sesame oil
10-inch piece cucumber, thinly sliced diagonally, then cut into long matchsticks
For the peanut sauce:
8 tbsp peanut butter
6 tbsp sugar
4 tbsp vinegar
5 tbsp chicken stock (see page 25)
3 tbsp light soy sauce
1 tbsp dark soy sauce
4 tsp sesame oil
3–4 tsp chile oil

● Put the chicken in a large pan of water. Bring to a boil and simmer for 20 minutes, skimming off the scum from time to time. The poaching water can be put toward making stock. When the chicken is cooled, shred with your fingers or with a knife.
● Mix the peanut butter, sugar, vinegar, chicken stock, soy sauce, sesame oil, and chile oil together in a bowl.
● Bring a large pan of water to a boil, and add the noodles. Cook for 3 minutes, rinse, and drain. Toss the noodles in the sesame oil, then arrange them on individual plates.
● Place a quarter of the shredded chicken and cucumber onto each serving of noodles. Pour on the sesame sauce, and serve immediately.

Right
Chilled Egg Noodles with Chicken and Peanut Sauce

chilled udon with five toppings

Dried, medium-sized *udon* is preferable for this dish if you can obtain them. A nonstick omelet pan will help you to prepare the egg sheets, which should resemble thin pancakes.

14 oz dried or 1¼ lb parboiled fresh *udon*
2¼ cups dipping broth *(see page 26)*, **chilled**
For the toppings:
2 eggs
2 tsp sugar
1 tbsp vegetable oil
8 okra
salt
4 tsp dried *wakame* seaweed, soaked in warm water and drained
8 chunks imitation crabmeat, torn into shreds
handful alfalfa sprouts

● Boil plenty of water in a pan. Add the *udon* and cook 8–15 minutes for dried or 3 minutes for fresh noodles. Rinse, and put the *udon* into four shallow bowls.

● Mix the eggs and sugar together in a bowl. Heat the oil in a frying pan, and pour in a third of the egg mixture. When the egg starts bubbling, turn it over. (The method is the same as for making thin pancakes.) Repeat this and make two more egg sheets. Let them cool, and then cut in half and then into shreds.

● Sprinkle the salt over the okra on a chopping board, then roll the okra with salt to remove the fine down. Boil some water in a pan, and blanch the okra for just a minute before chopping finely.

● Arrange the shredded egg, okra, *wakame*, crabmeat shreds, and sprouts in separate groups on top of the *udon*.

● Just before eating, pour the chilled dipping broth over the noodles.

chilled udon with fermented soybeans

Fermented soybeans, or *natto*, are not to everyone's taste. Even in Japan, where it originated, *natto* is very much a "love it or hate it" food, despite it being a nutritious source of protein. Give it a try. You never know—you might like it! *Natto* is available from Japanese food stores.

14 oz dried or 1¼ lb parboiled fresh *udon*
2¼ cups dipping broth *(see page 26)*, **chilled**
For the topping:
6 okra
salt
½ lb Japanese fermented soybeans (*natto*)
scant ⅓ cup bonito flakes (*katsuo bushi*)
1 scallion, chopped
1 tsp hot prepared mustard
4 tsp Japanese soy sauce
½ sheet *nori* seaweed, shredded

● Remove the tiny hairs on the okra; the easiest way to do this is to first sprinkle the salt over the okra, and then roll them over on a chopping board. Blanch in the boiling water for 1 minute, then drain and chop.

● Mix the okra, *natto*, bonito flakes, scallion, mustard, and soy sauce together in a bowl.

● Bring plenty of water to a boil in a large pan, and add the *udon*. Cook according to the instructions on the package. Rinse and drain. Divide the *udon* into four bowls.

● Pile the *natto* mixture on top of the udon. Gently pour the dipping broth into each bowl, sprinkle with *nori,* then serve immediately.

Right
Chilled Udon with Fermented Soybeans

chilled udon with eggplant and miso sauce

Miso sauce is a versatile performer that can be paired with almost any vegetable you care to mention. Here it is combined with eggplant, which should be soaked in salted water to remove any trace of bitterness.

2¼ cups dashi broth *(see page 26)*
4 tbsp vinegar
14 oz dried or 1¼ lb parboiled fresh udon
For the topping:
1 tbsp sunflower oil
2 cloves garlic, finely chopped
½-inch piece fresh ginger, peeled and finely chopped
8 scallions, chopped
½ lb eggplant, cut into matchstick-sized pieces and soaked in salted water
1 small green pepper, cut into matchstick-sized pieces
a pinch of salt
4 tbsp miso paste
1 tbsp Japanese soy sauce
2 tsp sugar
3 tbsp Japanese rice wine (sake)

● Mix the *dashi* broth and vinegar, then refrigerate. Heat the oil in a frying pan. Add the garlic, ginger, and scallion, and fry for 1 minute.

● Add the eggplant, green pepper, and salt, and stir-fry for 4–5 minutes, or until the eggplant is softened. Add the *miso* paste, soy sauce, sugar, and *sake,* and stir well. Set aside.

● Boil plenty of water in a pan, and add the *udon.* Cook for 4–5 minutes for fresh or 8–15 minutes for dried *udon,* or according to the instructions on the package. Rinse with cold water. Drain and divide into four bowls.

● Place the eggplant mixture on the *udon,* and pour the broth over the top. Serve immediately.

Right
Chilled Udon *with Eggplant and* Miso *Sauce*

chilled soba with nameko mushrooms

A light, refreshing lunch or part of a dinner that is quickly prepared and easily digested.

14 oz dried *soba*
approx 14 oz canned *nameko* mushrooms
¾ lb *mooli* or *daikon*, peeled and grated
½ sheet *nori* seaweed, shredded
2¼ cups dipping broth (see page 26), **chilled**

● Boil plenty of water in a large pan and add the *soba*. Cook for 5–6 minutes, or according to the instructions on the package. Rinse with plenty of cold water, and drain well. Divide the *soba* into four bowls.

● Mix the mushrooms and *mooli* or *daikon* together in a bowl. Pile them onto the *soba,* and sprinkle with the *nori*. Gently pour the chilled dipping broth over the top just before serving.

chilled soba with bean curd sheet

A refreshing summertime treat. There is nothing quite like chilled *soba* and a good dipping broth to restore heat-jaded appetites.

14 oz dried *soba*
2¼ cups dipping broth (see page 26), **chilled**
For the topping:
2 bean curd sheet (*abura-age*)
1 tbsp vegetable oil
8 *shiitake* mushrooms, sliced
salt and pepper
2 tsp soy sauce
2 generous handfuls alfalfa sprouts
3 scallions, chopped

● Pierce two sides of the *abura-age* with skewers, and grill directly over a gas ring or broil for about 50 seconds on each side. Slice into thin strips, and set aside.

● Heat the oil in a pan and fry the mushrooms for about 2 minutes. Season with salt and pepper, and sprinkle with the soy sauce. Set aside.

● Bring plenty of water to a boil in a large saucepan. Add the *soba,* and cook for 5–6 minutes. Drain, and rinse well under cold running water. Drain again, and divide into four portions.

● Mix the *abura-age*, mushrooms, and sprouts together well in a bowl. Divide among the four servings, and sprinkle with scallions. Pour the broth over the top just before serving.

chilled soba with soured plum sauce

The bite of the soured plums in the dipping broth gives an extra zest to this cold noodle dish.

4 scallions, sliced
3 boneless chicken breasts
12 okra
salt
14 oz dried *soba*
For the sour plum sauce:
4 large soured plums (*umeboshi*), seeded and chopped finely
2¼ cups dipping broth (see page 26)

● Soak the sliced scallions in cold water until ready for use. Cook the chicken in boiling water for about 15 minutes, or until cooked. When cooled, pull the meat into small strips with your fingers.

● Sprinkle the okra with salt, then roll each on a chopping board to remove the fine hairs. Cook for around a minute in boiling water, then cut into ½-inch slices.

● Put the soured plums into a mortar. Add a little broth and grind roughly into a thin paste. Return the mixture to the dipping broth, and then chill in the refrigerator.

● Bring plenty of water to a boil in a large saucepan. Add the *soba,* and cook for 5–6 minutes. Drain, and rinse well under cold running water. Drain again. Mix the *soba* with the scallions in a bowl, and then divide into four portions.

● Add the chicken and okra. Pour the soured plum dipping broth over the top, and serve at once.

Left

Chilled

Soba with

Nameko

Mushrooms

chilled soba with deep-fried mackerel

Mackerel is one of the great mainstays of the Japanese diet. It is not only eaten raw as *sushi* and *sashimi,* but is incorporated in many Japanese cooked dishes, as here.

14 oz dried *soba*
2¼ cups dipping broth
  (see page 26)
For the topping:
vegetable oil for deep frying
8 tbsp flour
½ cup water
1 lb mackerel, gutted, filleted,
  and cut into four pieces per
  person
¾ lb *mooli* or *daikon*, peeled and
  grated
2 scallions, chopped
alfalfa sprouts to garnish

● Heat the vegetable oil in a saucepan to 350°F. Mix the flour and water lightly in a bowl to a lumpy consistency to make a batter, then dip the mackerel pieces in. Deep fry for about 3 minutes, or until golden brown.

● Bring plenty of water to a boil in a large saucepan. Add the *soba,* and cook for 5–6 minutes. Drain, and rinse well under cold running water. Drain again, and then divide into four portions.

● Place four pieces of deep-fried mackerel in each bowl. Place the grated *mooli* or *daikon* in the center and garnish with the scallions and sprouts. Pour the dipping broth over the top, and serve immediately.

chilled soba with shredded daikon

Japanese *daikon* is the ideal ingredient for this dish, but is hard to come by unless there happens to be a Japanese food store nearby. I find that *mooli* makes an acceptable stand-in, or, failing that, try radishes.

14 oz dried *soba*
¾ lb *daikon* or *mooli*, peeled and
  shredded
handful alfalfa sprouts
1 sheet *nori* seaweed, shredded
3 cups dipping broth
  (see page 26)
For the garnishes:
2 scallions, chopped
1-inch piece fresh ginger, grated
2 *myoga* (optional), shredded

● Bring plenty of water to a boil in a large saucepan. Add the soba, and cook for 5–6 minutes. Rinse and cool in cold water. Drain.

● Mix the *soba, daikon,* and sprouts well in a bowl. Divide into individual serving bowls, and sprinkle with the *nori.* Serve with the chilled dipping broth and garnishes on a separate small dish.

Right
Chilled Soba
with
Shredded
Daikon

classic cold somen

A cool, refreshing, and easily digested dish for those hot summer days when you just can't face eating anything hot or heavy.

1 lb somen
3 cups chilled dipping broth
  (see page 26)
For the garnish:
1 sheet nori, seaweed, shredded
3 scallions, chopped
2 tsp wasabi horseradish
8 leaves Bowles' mint (oba),
  shredded
ice cubes

● Put the *somen* noodles into a pan of boiling water. When the water returns to the boil, add ½ cup water to reduce the temperature again. The second time the water comes back to a boil, the *somen* will be ready. Drain well, and rinse with cold water. Drain again.

● Place the ice cubes on a serving platter, and pile all the *somen* on top of the ice to keep it cool. Each diner takes *somen* as required using chopsticks. Serve the dipping broth cold in small cups or bowls, with the garnish also served on small, individual dishes.

How to eat
somen

Place some of the garnish into your dipping broth, then take some of the *somen* from the serving platter with your chopsticks, dip into the broth, then slurp it up with your lips.

Left *Classic Cold Somen*

chilled soba with vegetable tempura

Tempura, or deep-fried vegetables, are one of the most famous Japanese dishes. Both the *tempura* and *soba* should be dipped into the broth as you eat this dish.

vegetable oil for deep frying
For the batter:
1 egg, beaten
9 tbsp flour
1 cup cold water
6 oz eggplant, halved and sliced
4 shiitake mushrooms
4–5 small carrots, cut into long
  matchsticks
16 green beans
14 oz dried soba
3 cups chilled dipping broth
  (see page 26)

● Fill a saucepan ⅓ full with the oil, and heat to 350°F. Mix the egg, flour, and water lightly in a bowl. Dip the eggplant and *shiitake* mushrooms in the batter, then deep fry until golden. Dip the carrots and green beans in the batter in small bundles, and deep fry. Drain on paper towels.

● Boil plenty of water in a pan, add the *soba*, and cook for 4–6 minutes or according to the instructions on the package. Rinse, and drain well.

● Put the *soba* on four plates, and divide the *tempura* onto four separate plates. Fill four small cups with the dipping broth. Serve at once.

chilled somen with sesame dipping

Fried vegetables make the chilled *somen* more nutritious and filling, while the combination of the sesame sauce and dipping broth imparts a rich and delicate flavor. It is a good idea to make the dipping broth in advance; it will keep in the refrigerator for a few days.

14 oz *somen*
For the sesame dipping broth:
2¼ cups dipping broth
  (see page 26)
½-inch piece fresh ginger, peeled
  and squeezed for the juice
5 tbsp sesame sauce
2 scallions, finely chopped
For the topping:
sunflower oil for frying
¾ lb eggplant, thinly sliced and
  soaked in salted water
4 large *shiitake* mushrooms
1 small green pepper
4 *myoga* (optional), finely
  chopped

● Heat the dipping broth, and add the ginger juice and sesame sauce. When it comes to a boil, add the scallions and turn off the heat. Refrigerate.
● Bring plenty of water to a boil in a pan, and add the *somen*. When the water returns to a boil, add half a cup of cold water. The second time the water comes back to a boil, the *somen* will be ready. Rinse with the cold water, and drain. Put the *somen* onto four plates.
● Heat 2 tablespoons of oil in a frying pan. Fry the eggplant slices first, then the mushrooms and pepper. If you need more oil, add another 2 tablespoons.
● Place the eggplant, mushrooms, and pepper beside the *somen*, and, if using, put the sliced *myoga* on top. Serve immediately with small bowls of dipping broth.

chilled somen with pork

An invigorating combination of chilled noodles with pork and broccoli stir-fried in a hot *toban* sauce.

14 oz *somen*
2¼ cups dipping broth
  (see page 26), chilled
For the topping:
1½ tbsp vegetable oil
4 cloves garlic, sliced
¾ lb lean pork, sliced on a slant
  into bite-sized pieces
1 tbsp *mirin*
2½ tbsp soy sauce
2 tsp chile bean sauce
  (toban djan)
8 small broccoli florets
a pinch of salt

● Heat the oil in a pan, then add the garlic and fry for about a minute. Add the meat, and fry for a further 2–3 minutes. Then add the *mirin*, soy sauce, and chile bean sauce, and stir-fry for 2 minutes.
● Bring plenty of water to a boil in a large saucepan. Add the *somen*, and cook for 1–2 minutes. Drain, and rinse well under cold running water. Drain again, and then divide into four portions.
● Meanwhile, bring a pan of water to a boil, add a pinch of salt, and boil the broccoli for 1–2 minutes. Drain and rinse.
● Place the meat and broccoli in the four bowls. Serve immediately after pouring in the chilled dipping broth.

Right
Chilled
Somen
with Pork

[76]

bean-thread noodle salad with barbecued pork

The secret of success with this dish is to have good quality pork well marinated in *cha siu* sauce, and then roast it long enough to be edible, but not so long as to overcook the center of the meat.

½ lb bean-thread noodles
4–5 small carrots, cut into
  matchsticks
½ lb cucumber, cut into
  matchsticks
½ lb Chinese barbecued pork
  (*cha siu*) (see page 34), shredded
2 dried black ear fungi, soaked
  and shredded, or 2–3 *shiitake*
  mushrooms (optional)
4 tsp toasted sesame seeds
  (see page 63)
For the dressing:
4 tbsp light soy sauce
2½ tbsp dark soy sauce
2½ tbsp sugar
5 tbsp vinegar
4 tbsp sesame oil

● Soak the bean-thread noodles in warm water for 5 minutes, or according to the instructions on the package. Rinse under water, and drain.
● Mix the soy sauce, sugar, vinegar, and sesame oil together in a bowl. Add the carrots, cucumber, *cha siu* pork, black ear fungus, or mushrooms, if using, and noodles, and mix well.
● Serve the noodles either on a large dish or in four individual dishes, and sprinkle with toasted sesame seeds before eating.

bean-thread noodle salad with shrimp

yam woonsen

Yam woonsen is a hot Thai salad. *Nam pla*, an essential ingredient used in Thai cuisine, enhances the flavor of the dish. It is a good idea to prepare this salad at least 30 minutes before you serve it to allow the full sweet, hot flavor to mature.

½ lb bean-thread noodles
16 tiger shrimp, peeled and
  deveined
1 tsp fish sauce (*nam pla*)
2 tsp freshly squeezed lemon
  juice
1 tsp palm or brown sugar
1 tbsp sunflower oil
1 small red pepper, finely
  chopped
2 stalks celery, thinly sliced
4–5 small carrots, cut into
  matchsticks
2 scallions, chopped
4–5 lettuce leaves
cilantro leaves to garnish
For the dressing:
2 shallots, finely chopped
1 dry red chile, crushed
3 small green chile, chopped
4 tbsp fish sauce (*nam pla*)
½ cup freshly squeezed lemon
  juice (about 2 lemons)
4½ tbsp palm or brown sugar
1 tbsp sunflower oil

● Soak the bean-thread noodles in warm water for 5 minutes, or according to the instructions on the package. Rinse under cold running water, and drain.
● Marinate the shrimp in 1 teaspoon fish sauce, 2 teaspoons of lemon juice, and 1 teaspoon sugar for 15 minutes.
● Meanwhile, mix together the dressing ingredients.
● Heat 1 tablespoon oil in a frying pan, and stir-fry the shrimp thoroughly.
● Put the red pepper, celery, carrot, scallions, and noodles in a bowl, and mix together. Place a lettuce leaf on each plate, and pile the noodle mixture onto it. Put the shrimp on the noodles, and sprinkle with the cilantro leaves.

Right

*Bean-
Thread
Noodle
Salad with
Shrimp*

stir- fried noodles

Chow mein must be the most famous stir-fried noodle dish in the west. This quick method using a wok creates mouthwatering noodle dishes in minutes. Stir-fried egg noodles, rice noodles, or udon are widely eaten in southeast Asia, each country adding its own particular flavoring.

stir-fried egg noodles with barbecued pork

Literally translated as "stir-fried noodles," *chow mein* is an archetypal noodle fast-food, and one of the first noodle dishes to become popularized in the West.

1 lb fresh or 10 oz dried thin
   egg noodles
2 tbsp vegetable oil
1-inch piece fresh ginger,
   peeled and finely chopped
2 cloves garlic, finely chopped
1 medium onion, sliced
3 medium carrots, sliced into
   bite-sized pieces
12 snowpeas, blanched
3 cups bean sprouts, rinsed
½ lb Chinese barbecued pork
   (*cha siu*) (*see page 34*), sliced
   and cut into bite-sized
   squares
1 tbsp sesame oil
4 tbsp light soy sauce
1 tbsp dark soy sauce
1 tbsp sugar
salt and black pepper

● Boil plenty of water in a pan, and cook the noodles for 3 minutes. Rinse under running water, and drain.

● Heat the vegetable oil in a wok or frying pan until very hot. Stir-fry the ginger and garlic for 30 seconds. Add the onion, carrots, and snowpeas, and stir-fry for 2 minutes. Add the bean sprouts and *cha siu* pork, and stir-fry for another 2 minutes.

● Add the sesame oil, noodles, soy sauce, and sugar, and stir-fry for 1 minute until the noodles are coated with sauce. Season if necessary, and stir once more. Serve immediately.

stir-fried egg noodles with yakisoba sauce

Maybe the most popular noodle dish eaten in Japan, this is found in noodle shops, at home, and is made and served in the street, at festivals, or cooked over a campfire for lunch during a trip out into the countryside. If *yakisoba* sauce is unavailable, make your own (see page 88).

¾ lb dried egg noodles or 1¼ lb
   Japanese steamed noodles
1 tbsp sesame oil
2 tbsp sunflower oil
½ lb boneless belly of pork or
   chicken breasts, thinly sliced
1 medium-sized onion, sliced
4–5 small carrots, cut in half
   lengthwise and thinly sliced
5 cabbage leaves, cut roughly
salt and black pepper
7 tbsp *yakisoba* or Japanese
   brown sauce
***nori* seaweed flakes (*ao-nori*)**
   (optional)
red pickled ginger (*beni-shouga*)
   (optional)

● If using dried noodles, boil plenty of water in a pan, add the noodles, and cook for 3 minutes. Rinse with water and drain. Toss the noodles in the sesame oil. If you use Japanese steamed noodles, just rinse with very hot water.

● Heat the sunflower oil in a wok or frying pan, then fry the pork or chicken for 3–4 minutes. Add the onions, carrots, and cabbage, and stir-fry for 3–4 minutes. Sprinkle with the salt and pepper, add the noodles and *yakisoba* or brown sauce, and stir well.

● Put the noodles onto four plates, and sprinkle with the *nori* flakes and pickled ginger. Serve at once.

Right
Stir-fried Egg Noodles with Yakisoba Sauce

stir-fried egg noodles with vegetables

chow mein with vegetables

1 lb fresh or 10 oz dried
  medium egg noodles
2 tbsp vegetable oil
1-inch piece fresh ginger,
  peeled and finely chopped
2 cloves garlic, finely chopped
10 oz Chinese cabbage,
  chopped into bite-sized
  squares
2½ cups bean sprouts
1 small red pepper, cut into
  bite-sized squares
1 small green pepper, cut into
  bite-sized squares
16 straw mushrooms (canned),
  halved
1 tbsp sesame oil
2 scallions, chopped
4 tbsp light soy sauce
1 tbsp dark soy sauce
1 tbsp sugar
salt and black pepper

● Boil plenty of water in a pan, and cook the noodles for 3–4 minutes. Rinse under cold water, and drain.

● Heat the vegetable oil in a wok or frying pan, then stir-fry the ginger and garlic for 30 seconds. Add the Chinese cabbage, bean sprouts, red and green peppers, and straw mushrooms. Stir each ingredient as you add it. Fry together for about 2 minutes.

● Add the sesame oil, noodles, scallions, soy sauce, and sugar, and stir well. Check the taste, adding salt and pepper if necessary. Put the noodles onto four plates and serve immediately.

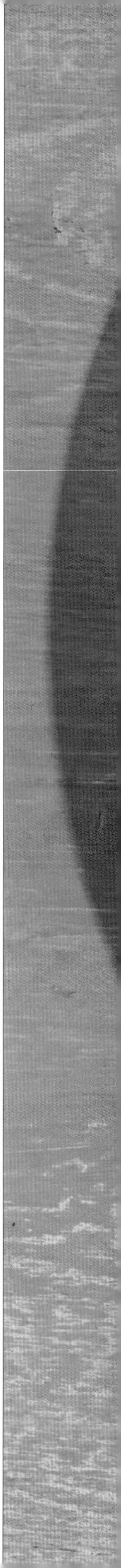

Right

*Stir-fried
Egg
Noodles
with
Vegetables*

stir-fried egg noodles with shrimp and black bean sauce

These stir-fried noodles require cooking for only a short time. Tiger shrimp add both flavor and a certain luxury to this dish, so if you are feeling extravagant, use them in place of their smaller cousins.

1 lb fresh or 10 oz dried medium egg noodles
3 tbsp vegetable oil
1-inch piece fresh ginger, peeled and finely chopped
3 cloves garlic, finely chopped
¼ lb peeled shrimp
12 tiger or jumbo shrimp, peeled and deveined
1 small red pepper, sliced
4 scallions, chopped into 1-inch lengths
black pepper
1 tbsp sesame oil
4 tsp light soy sauce
4 tsp dark soy sauce
2 tbsp Chinese rice wine or dry sherry
3 tbsp black bean sauce

● Cook the noodles in a pan of boiling water for 4 minutes. Rinse, and drain well.

● Heat the vegetable oil in a wok or frying pan. Stir-fry the ginger and garlic for 30 seconds. Add the shrimp, red pepper, scallions, and a sprinkling of black pepper, and stir for 1–2 minutes or until the shrimp are heated thoroughly.

● Add the sesame oil and noodles, and stir. Add the soy sauce, rice wine, and black bean sauce, then stir again until the noodles are coated well with the sauce.

● Put the noodles onto four plates, and serve at once.

Malaysian spicy egg noodles

This dish uses *belacan*, the pungent shrimp-based paste commonly used in Malaysian and Thai cooking. Don't let the odor put you off when you use *belacan*, but be warned that the aroma does tend to stick around unless you ensure your kitchen is well-ventilated while you are cooking!

10 oz dried medium egg noodles
5 tbsp vegetable oil
4–6 small dried red chiles, soaked in hot water, then ground
2 cloves garlic, finely chopped
1 tsp dried shrimp paste (belacan) (optional)
10 oz rump steak, thinly sliced
1 medium-sized onion, thinly sliced
2 green chiles, chopped
2½ cups bean sprouts
¼ lb mustard greens or fresh spinach
salt and black pepper
3 tbsp light soy sauce
cilantro leaves
4 lime wedges

● Boil plenty of water in a pan, and cook the noodles for 4 minutes. Rinse under water, and drain. Set aside.

● Heat 3 tablespoons of the oil in a wok or frying pan. Add the chiles, garlic, and *belacan*, and stir. Add the beef, and fry for 2–3 minutes.

● Add the onion, green chiles, bean sprouts, and mustard greens, stirring each time you add the ingredients. Season with salt and pepper.

● Add the remaining oil and the egg noodles, sprinkle soy sauce over the mixture, and mix all the ingredients well. Put the noodles onto four plates, and garnish with cilantro leaves and lime wedges. Serve at once.

Right

Malaysian
Spicy Egg
Noodles

Indonesian fried egg noodles with chicken and bean curd

mie goreng

Indonesian cooking has become increasingly popular over the last few years, and *mie goreng*, one of the most commonly eaten dishes in Indonesia, has been at the forefront of this trend.

10 oz dried medium egg noodles
4 tbsp + 2 tsp vegetable oil
10 oz bean curd (*tofu*), diced
2 eggs, beaten
1-inch piece fresh ginger, peeled and finely chopped
4 shallots, finely chopped
1 tsp ground coriander seeds
1 red chile, chopped
½ lb boneless chicken breasts, diced
4–5 small carrots, sliced
3 stalks celery, sliced
4 scallions, chopped into 1-inch lengths
3 tbsp light soy sauce
salt and pepper
4 tomato wedges
sliced cucumber

● Cook the egg noodles in a pan of boiling water for 4 minutes. Rinse, and drain well.

● Heat 1 tablespoon of the oil in a wok or frying pan, and fry the bean curd until lightly browned. Set aside, and clean the wok.

● To make the egg sheets, heat 1 teaspoon of the oil in an omelet pan. Add half the beaten egg and fry both sides, like a thin pancake. Repeat to make a second egg sheet. When the egg sheets are cooled, slice them thinly.

● Heat another 2 tablespoons of the oil in the wok, stir-fry the ginger, shallots, ground coriander, and red chile for 30 seconds. Add the chicken, and stir for 2–3 minutes. Add the carrots, celery, bean curd, and scallions, stirring each time you add the ingredients.

● Add 1 tablespoon of the oil, the egg noodles, and soy sauce to the wok, and stir well. Divide the noodles onto four plates, sprinkle the sliced egg sheets on top, and garnish with tomato wedges and cucumber slices. Serve at once.

stir-fried udon with yakisoba sauce

If you cannot obtain *yakisoba* sauce or Japanese brown sauce, try making your own (see box).

1½ lb parboiled fresh or 14 oz dried *udon*
3 tbsp sunflower oil
½ lb ground pork
1 medium-sized onion, sliced
½ lb Chinese cabbage, sliced
½ red pepper, sliced
6 oz snowpeas, cut in half
salt and black pepper

8 tbsp *yakisoba* or Japanese brown sauce
***nori* seaweed flakes (*ao-nori*) (optional)**
red pickled ginger (*beni-shouga*) (optional)

● Rinse the parboiled *udon* with very hot water or, if using dried *udon*, cook according to the instructions on the package.

● Heat the oil in a wok or frying pan until very hot. Add the pork and fry for 3 minutes. Add the onion, Chinese cabbage, red pepper, and snowpeas, and stir-fry for about 3 minutes. Season with salt and pepper.

● Add the *udon* and *yakisoba* or Japanese brown sauce, and stir well. Divide the *udon* onto four plates. Sprinkle *nori* flakes and pickled ginger over the top, and serve.

yakisoba sauce

5–6 servings
5 tbsp brown sauce
4 tbsp light soy sauce
4 tsp tomato catsup
4 tsp oyster sauce
4 tbsp sugar
Mix all the ingredients together

Right

Indonesian fried egg noodles with chicken and bean card

stir-fried udon with seafood

Stir-frying coaxes maximum flavor out of the seafood ingredients, and gives the *udon* noodles a smooth, slippery texture in this filling dish.

14 oz dried or 1¼ lb parboiled fresh *udon*
3 tbsp sunflower oil
6 oz squid, cleaned and sliced
6 oz peeled shrimp
4 scallions, chopped roughly
3 cups bean sprouts
10 oz *shimeji* mushrooms, roots cut off and separated, or 15 *shiitake* mushrooms, sliced
4 tsp dried *wakame* seaweed, soaked in hot water
4 tbsp bonito flakes (*katsuobushi*)
4 tbsp Japanese soy sauce
salt and black pepper

● Boil plenty of water in a large pan, and add the *udon*. Cook for 7–15 minutes for dried, or 3 minutes for parboiled fresh *udon*. Rinse with cold water, and drain.
● Heat the oil in a wok or frying pan until very hot. Stir-fry the squid and shrimp for 2 minutes. Add the scallions, bean sprouts, mushrooms, and *wakame*, and stir-fry for about 2 minutes.
● Add the *udon*, bonito flakes, and soy sauce, and stir. Season with salt and pepper. Stir for another minute, and serve at once.

stir-fried udon with curry sauce

This is a rather *nouveau* way of cooking *udon* in Japan. However, hot *udon* soup with curry sauce is very popular, which must prove that curry and *udon* make a good combination.

1¼ lb parboiled fresh or 14 oz dried *udon*
4 tbsp sunflower oil
1 large clove garlic, finely chopped
1 medium-sized onion, sliced
1 small red pepper, sliced
¾ lb eggplant, quartered lengthwise and sliced into ½-inch wedges
1½ cups button mushrooms, sliced
For the sauce:
2 tbsp hot water
½ vegetable or chicken stock cube, crumbled
4 tbsp tomato catsup
1–2 tsp hot curry powder
½ tsp salt
cilantro leaves to garnish

● Boil plenty of water in a large pan, and add the *udon*. Cook dried *udon* according to the instructions on the package, and fresh *udon* for 3 minutes. Rinse under cold water, and drain.
● Heat the oil in a wok or frying pan until very hot. Add the garlic and onion, and stir-fry for 1 minute. Then add the red pepper, eggplant, and mushrooms, and stir-fry for about 4–5 minutes or until the eggplant has softened.
● Mix the hot water, stock cube, tomato catsup, curry powder, and salt together in a bowl to make a curry sauce. Add the *udon* and curry mixture to the vegetables, and stir-fry for a further 1–2 minutes. Garnish with the cilantro leaves, and serve immediately.

Right
Stir-fried
Udon *with*
Curry
Sauce

stir-fried rice vermicelli with liver and chives

Rice vermicelli is light and easy to digest. This Chinese recipe is usually served as a light lunch dish. As the liver is marinated in rice wine and soy sauce, its taste, which some people find offputting, is reduced. You can use any type of liver, though this recipe uses chicken.

½ **lb rice vermicelli**
1 lb chicken liver, sliced
2 tsp light soy sauce
1 tsp Chinese rice wine or dry sherry
1 tbsp cornstarch
3 tbsp vegetable oil
2 cloves garlic, finely chopped
1-inch piece fresh ginger, peeled and finely chopped
3 cups bean sprouts
8 dried *shiitake* mushrooms, soaked in hot water, then sliced
½ lb Chinese green chives or scallions, cut into 2-inch lengths
salt
For the sauce:
1 tbsp sesame oil
4 tbsp chicken stock *(see page 25)*
1 tbsp Chinese rice wine or dry sherry
2½ tbsp light soy sauce
4 tsp dark soy sauce
2 tsp oyster sauce
1 tsp sugar
black pepper

● Soak the vermicelli in warm water for 3 minutes, or according to the instructions on the package. Rinse under cold water, and drain. Blanch the liver in boiling water until it turns white. Then marinate the liver in the soy sauce, rice wine, and cornstarch for about 20 minutes.

● Heat 2 tablespoons of the oil in a wok or frying pan. Stir-fry the liver for 3–4 minutes before adding the garlic and ginger. Stir well. Add the remaining tablespoon of oil, the bean sprouts, mushrooms, and green chives or scallions, and stir-fry for 1–2 minutes.

● Add sauce ingredients and the vermicelli, and stir until the sauce is all absorbed. Taste, and season with salt if required. Divide the noodles between four plates, and serve at once.

stir-fried udon with miso sauce

This is another *nouveau* stir-fried *udon* dish. The *udon* are coated in a salty sauce, making a very appetising fast meal.

14 oz dried or 1¼ lb parboiled fresh *udon*
½ lb green cabbage
½ lb fresh green beans
3 tbsp sunflower oil
½ lb rump steak, sliced on a slant into bite-sized pieces
1 small red pepper, chopped into bite-sized pieces
10 *shiitake* mushrooms, quartered
a pinch of salt and chile powder
2 tbsp red *miso* paste
2 tbsp Japanese soy sauce
2 tbsp *mirin*
1 scallion, chopped

● Boil plenty of water in a large pan, and cook dried *udon* for 7–15 minutes or parboiled fresh *udon* for 3 minutes. Rinse, and drain.

● Blanch the cabbage leaves and green beans for 2 minutes. Rinse under cold water. Cut the cabbage leaves into bite-sized pieces, and halve the green beans.

● Heat the oil in a wok or frying pan until very hot. Add the beef, and fry for 2–3 minutes. Add the cabbage, green beans, and *shiitake* mushrooms, and sprinkle on salt and chile powder. Stir-fry for another 2–3 minutes.

● Mix the *miso*, soy sauce, and *mirin* together in a bowl. Add the *udon* and *miso* mixture to the pan, and stir-fry for about a minute. Put the *udon* onto four plates. Sprinkle with chopped scallions, and serve at once.

Right
Stir-fried Udon *with* Miso *Sauce*

Thai fried vermicelli with red curry paste

Thai red curry paste is a result of the influence of Indian and Chinese cooking. The result is a novel and interesting combination of heat and sourness.

½ lb rice vermicelli
3 tbsp vegetable oil
½ lb bean curd (*tofu*) diced
3 cloves garlic, chopped
4 oz canned bamboo shoots
3 cups bean sprouts
¼ lb mustard greens or fresh
  spinach
2 tbsp Thai red curry paste
6 tbsp fish sauce (*nam pla*)
3 tbsp light soy sauce
I tbsp palm or brown sugar
cilantro leaves
4 lime wedges

● Soak the rice vermicelli in warm water for 3–5 minutes. Rinse, and drain.

● Heat the oil in a wok or frying pan, and fry the bean curd until golden brown. Add the garlic, bamboo shoots, bean sprouts, and mustard greens or spinach, stirring each time you add the ingredients.

● Add the red curry paste, fish sauce, soy sauce, and brown sugar, then stir well. Add the vermicelli, and stir until the noodles are well coated with sauce.

● Put the vermicelli onto four plates, and garnish with cilantro leaves and lime wedges. Serve at once.

stir-fried rice vermicelli with barbecued pork and shrimp

Another Chinese noodle dish using *cha siu* to provide extra flavor. If you do not have time to make *cha siu*, you can use sliced lean pork instead.

½ lb rice vermicelli
4 tbsp vegetable oil
I-inch piece fresh ginger, peeled
  and finely chopped
2 cloves garlic, finely chopped
½ lb Chinese barbecued pork
  (*cha siu*) (*see page 34*), diced
¼ lb peeled shrimp
2½ cups bean sprouts
8 water chestnuts, sliced
6 scallions, chopped
¼ lb spinach, chopped
2 tbsp Chinese rice wine or dry
  sherry
4 tbsp light soy sauce
I½ tbsp dark soy sauce
6 tbsp chicken stock (*see page 25*)
black pepper and salt

● Soak the vermicelli in warm water for 3 minutes, or according to the instructions on the package. Rinse under running water, and drain.

● Heat 3 tablespoons of the oil in a wok or large frying pan until very hot. Stir-fry the ginger and garlic for 30 seconds. Add the pork, shrimp, bean sprouts, water chestnuts, scallions, and spinach, and stir-fry for 2–3 minutes.

● Add the remaining tablespoon of oil and the vermicelli, stir quickly, then add the rice wine, soy sauce, and chicken stock. Keep stirring until the sauce is absorbed. Sprinkle with black pepper and salt to taste. Serve immediately.

Right
Stir-fried Rice Vermicelli with Barbecued Pork and Shrimp

Singapore spicy noodles

The return home of itinerant Chinese over the years has resulted in a gradual increase in the popularity of curried dishes in China, especially in the south-western provinces. Although the origins of this dish lie in India, Singapore has been the cultural melting pot where most Chinese migrants have come into contact with Indian cuisine.

½ **lb rice vermicelli**
4 tbsp vegetable oil
2 cloves garlic, finely chopped
½**-inch piece fresh ginger, peeled and finely chopped**
1 red chile, chopped
¼ **lb peeled shrimp**
6 small squid, cleaned and sliced
3 cups bean sprouts
¼ **lb spinach**
½ **lb Chinese barbecued pork (cha siu)** *(see page 34)*, **thinly sliced**
2 eggs, beaten
3 scallions, roughly chopped
⅔ **tsp salt**
a pinch of chile powder
black pepper
2–3 tsp hot curry powder
1 tbsp light soy sauce
2 tsp sugar
⅔ **cup chicken stock** *(see page 25)*

● Soak the rice vermicelli in warm water for 3 minutes, or according to the instructions on the package. Rinse with cold water, and drain.
● Heat 3 tablespoons of the oil in a wok or frying pan until very hot. Add the garlic, ginger, and red chile, and stir-fry for 30 seconds.
● Add the shrimp and squid, and stir for another minute. Then add the bean sprouts, spinach, and pork, and stir-fry for 1–2 minutes.
● Make a well in the center, add the beaten egg, and scramble lightly. Quickly add the remaining tablespoon of oil and the rice vermicelli, and mix all the ingredients well.
● Add the scallions, salt, chile powder, black pepper, curry powder, soy sauce, sugar, and chicken stock. Stir until the sauce is absorbed. Put the noodles onto four plates, and serve at once.

Right
Singapore Spicy Noodles

Indonesian fried vermicelli with squid

Squid is a great favorite throughout Asia, and nowhere more so than in Indonesia. The flavorings used here are distinct, but without being so powerful as to cloak the taste of the seafood.

½ **lb rice vermicelli**
3 **tbsp vegetable oil**
1-**inch piece fresh ginger, peeled and finely chopped**
4 **shallots, chopped finely**
8 **small squid, cleaned and sliced**
4–5 **small carrots, cut into matchsticks**
2½ **cups bean sprouts**
¼ **lb fresh spinach, chopped**
1 **small red chile, chopped**
1 **tsp ground paprika**
3 **tbsp light soy sauce**
salt and black pepper
4 **tomato wedges**
sliced cucumber

● Soak the rice vermicelli in warm water for 3 minutes, or according to the instructions on the package. Rinse, and drain. Heat 2 tablespoons of the oil in a wok or frying pan, and stir-fry the ginger and shallots for 30 seconds. Add the squid, and stir until the squid turns white.

● Add the carrots, bean sprouts, spinach, and chile, and stir for 1–2 minutes. Add the remaining tablespoon of oil, the vermicelli, paprika, and soy sauce, and stir well.

● Taste, and add the salt and black pepper if required. Put the vermicelli onto four plates, and garnish with the tomato wedges and sliced cucumber. Serve at once.

fried flat rice noodles with beef and black bean sauce

Black bean sauce is just one of a number of end products that result from the fermentation of soybeans. Prepared with salt and spices, the black bean forms the basis of a very distinctive sauce to complement most meats. Here it is used with beef, but you will find it makes an equally good companion to pork.

2 **lb fresh flat rice noodles, or 10 oz dried rice-stick noodles**
1 **lb rump steak, sliced at a slant into bite-sized pieces**
1 **egg white**
3 **tbsp Chinese rice wine or dry sherry**
4 **tbsp light soy sauce**
2 **tsp cornstarch**
7 **tbsp vegetable oil**
1-**inch piece fresh ginger, peeled and finely chopped**
3 **cloves garlic, finely chopped**
2 **scallions, chopped**
2 **medium-sized onions, cut into bite-sized squares**
1 **large green pepper, cut into bite-sized squares**
6 **tbsp black bean sauce**
2 **tsp sugar**

● Rinse fresh flat rice noodles with hot water, or soak dried noodles in warm water for 2–5 minutes. Rinse, and drain.

● Marinate the beef with 1 tablespoon of the rice wine, 1 tablespoon of the soy sauce, and the cornstarch for 30 minutes.

● Heat 3 tablespoons of the oil in a wok or frying pan. Fry the beef for 2–3 minutes, and set aside. Clean the wok before the next step.

● Heat 2 tablespoons of the oil in a wok, and stir-fry the ginger and garlic for 30 seconds. Add the scallions, onion, and green pepper, and stir until the onion becomes transparent.

● Return the beef and noodles to the wok. Add 2 tablespoons of the oil, plus the black bean sauce, soy sauce, rice wine, and sugar. Stir well, until all the ingredients are thoroughly mixed. Divide the noodles onto four plates, and serve.

Right
Fried Flat Rice Noodles with Beef and Black Bean Sauce

fried rice-stick noodles with bean curd and black bean sauce

Tofu, or bean curd, is prepared by cutting it into small cubes. Be careful when you do this as it is delicate stuff and prone to disintegrate if handled too roughly. Nutritious and healthy as it undoubtedly is, *tofu* will never win any awards for flavor, which is why its combination with the spicy, aromatic black bean sauce makes such a good pairing.

10 oz dried rice-stick noodles
4 tbsp vegetable oil
¾ lb bean curd (*tofu*), diced
1-inch piece fresh ginger, peeled
  and finely chopped
2 cloves garlic, finely chopped
½ green pepper, diced
½ red pepper, diced
½ yellow pepper, diced
5 scallions, chopped
6 tbsp black bean sauce
3 tbsp light soy sauce
2 tbsp Chinese rice wine or dry
  sherry
2 tsp sugar

● Soak the rice-stick noodles in warm water for 2–5 minutes, depending on the instructions on the package. Rinse, and drain.

● Heat 3 tablespoons of the oil in a wok or frying pan. Fry the bean curd until golden brown. Add the ginger and garlic, and stir. Add the peppers and scallions, and stir-fry for 1–2 minutes.

● Add the remaining oil, noodles, black bean sauce, soy sauce, rice wine, and sugar, then stir until the noodles are well coated with the sauce. Divide the noodles onto four plates, and serve at once.

Right
Fried Rice-Stick Noodles with Bean Curd and Black Bean Sauce

spicy rice-stick noodles with chicken

Authentic Thai spicy noodles are very, very hot. I have altered the amount of green chile used in this recipe to cool them down and save your taste buds! However, if you feel like increasing the spices, you can add more green chile if you dare.

2 lb fresh flat rice noodles or
   10 oz dried rice-stick noodles
5 tbsp vegetable oil
2 cloves garlic, finely chopped
4–6 small green chiles, chopped
½ lb boneless chicken breasts,
   sliced into bite-sized pieces
1¼ cups frozen green beans,
   halved
¼ lb mustard greens or fresh
   spinach
16 canned or fresh baby corn,
   each cut diagonally into 3
   pieces
4 tbsp fish sauce (nam pla)
2 tbsp dark soy sauce
2 tbsp light soy sauce
1 tbsp palm or brown sugar
2 small tomatoes, halved

● If you use fresh noodles, just rinse with warm water. Soak dried rice noodles in warm water for 2–5 minutes, or according to the instructions on the package. Rinse, and drain.
● Heat 3 tablespoons of the oil in a wok or frying pan until very hot. Stir-fry the garlic and green chile for 30 seconds, then add the chicken and fry for about 3 minutes.
● Add the green beans, mustard greens or spinach, and baby corn, stirring for 1–2 minutes. Add the remaining oil and the rice noodles, and stir. Then add the fish sauce, soy sauce, and sugar, and stir well.
● Garnish with the tomatoes, and serve at once.

Thai fried rice-stick noodles
pad thai

The most widely eaten and best known of all the noodle dishes of Thailand. Like all the best noodle dishes, *pad thai* is simply prepared and ready in minutes. The key to a tasty *pad thai* lies in the use of salty dried shrimp and roasted peanuts. You can adjust the amount of chile used depending on your liking for spiciness.

10 oz dried rice-stick noodles
12 jumbo shrimp with tails,
   peeled and deveined
5 tbsp vegetable oil
3 cloves garlic, finely chopped
4 shallots, sliced
2 eggs, beaten
2 tbsp roast peanuts, crushed
3–4 small green chiles, chopped
2 tbsp dried shrimp, chopped
2 scallions, chopped
2½ cups bean sprouts

2½ tbsp palm or brown sugar
6 tbsp fish sauce (nam pla)
½ cup freshly squeezed lemon
   juice
cilantro leaves
4 lime wedges
For the prawn marinade:
1 tsp freshly squeezed lemon
   juice
1 tsp fish sauce (nam pla)
½ tsp palm or brown sugar

● Soak the rice-stick noodles in warm water for 2–5 minutes, or according to the instructions on the package. Rinse, and drain.
● Marinate the shrimp in the lemon juice, fish sauce, and sugar for at least 15 minutes.
● Heat 2 tablespoons of the oil in a wok or frying pan, and stir-fry the garlic and shallots for 30 seconds. Make a well in the center and add the eggs, then lightly scramble without incorporating the garlic and shallots.
● Add the peanuts, chiles, dried shrimp, scallions, and bean sprouts, and stir.
● Add another 2 tablespoons of oil and the noodles, and stir. Add the sugar, fish sauce, and lemon juice, then stir until the noodles are well coated.
● Quickly heat the remaining tablespoon of oil in the wok, and fry the shrimp thoroughly. Put the noodles onto four plates. Lay the shrimp on top, and garnish with cilantro and lime wedges. Serve at once.

Right
Thai Fried
Rice-stick
Noodles

rice-stick noodles with pork and shrimp

This dish contains the three foundations of Thai flavoring: garlic, shallots, and chiles. Thai garlic tends to be small compared to its western counterpart, so if the cloves you have are on the large side, use just one.

10 oz dried rice-stick noodles
5 tbsp vegetable oil
2 cloves garlic, finely chopped
3 shallots, chopped
½ lb lean pork, sliced into small pieces
¼ lb peeled shrimp
4–6 small green chiles, chopped
2½ cups bean sprouts
8 canned or fresh baby corn, cut diagonally into bite-sized pieces
3 stalks celery, cut diagonally into bite-sized pieces
2 eggs, beaten
2½ tbsp palm or brown sugar
3½ tbsp tomato catsup
6 tbsp fish sauce (nam pla)
½ cup freshly squeezed lemon juice
cilantro leaves
4 lime wedges

● Soak the noodles in warm water for 2–5 minutes, or according to instructions. Rinse, then drain.
● Heat 3 tablespoons of the oil in a wok or frying pan, and stir-fry the garlic and shallots for 30 seconds. Add the pork and fry for about 3 minutes. Add the shrimp and green chiles, stirring for another minute, then add the bean sprouts, baby corn, and celery, and fry for another 2 minutes.
● Make a well in the center, then pour in the egg and scramble quickly. Add the remaining oil and the rice-stick noodles, then stir. Add the sugar, tomato catsup, fish sauce, and lemon juice, and stir well.
● Divide the noodles onto four plates, and garnish with cilantro and lime wedges.

fried rice noodles with coconut sauce

The coconut and its parent palm have a hallowed place in the Thai psyche. The coconut itself has a wide variety of culinary uses, while the palm is employed to make furniture, toys, and musical instruments. Canned coconut milk varies in its consistency depending on the brand. A thicker product produces the richest, smoothest flavor. Remember to shake the can well before opening.

10 oz dried rice-stick noodles
3 tbsp vegetable oil
2 cloves garlic, finely chopped
3 shallots, chopped
14 oz rump steak, thinly sliced
16 canned or fresh baby corn, cut diagonally
4 scallions, chopped
2 stalks celery, chopped
2½ cups bean sprouts
1⅔ cups canned coconut milk
2 tsp palm or brown sugar
4 tbsp fish sauce (nam pla)
3 tbsp freshly squeezed lemon juice
1 tbsp Thai red curry paste
cilantro leaves

● Soak the rice-stick noodles in warm water for 2–5 minutes, or follow the instructions on the package. Rinse, and drain.
● Heat the oil in a wok or frying pan, then stir-fry the garlic and shallots for 30 seconds. Add the beef and stir-fry for about 3 minutes, before adding the baby corn, scallions, celery, and bean sprouts.
● Add the coconut milk, sugar, fish sauce, lemon juice, and curry paste, and stir well until the sauce is absorbed into the noodles.
● Put the noodles onto four plates, sprinkle with cilantro leaves, and serve at once.

fried bean-thread noodles with bean curd

Bean curd is a favorite constituent of Thai cooking. This dish features fried bean curd. Like all other types of bean curd, it is best to use what you buy in one go as it quickly deteriorates, even if refrigerated.

½ lb bean-thread noodles
4 tbsp vegetable oil
10 oz bean curd (*tofu*), diced
3 cloves garlic, finely chopped
4 shallots, finely chopped
2½ cups bean sprouts
1¼ cups frozen green beans, halved
2 scallions, chopped
2 tbsp roast peanuts, crushed
2 tbsp dried shrimp, chopped
3–5 small green chiles, chopped
2½ tbsp palm or brown sugar
6 tbsp fish sauce (*nam pla*)
½ cup freshly squeezed lemon juice
For the garnish:
2 tbsp crispy onion (*see glossary*)
cilantro leaves
1 medium red chile, sliced
4 slices lime

● Soak the bean-thread noodles in boiling water for 5 minutes. Rinse under cold water, and drain. Heat half the oil in a wok or frying pan, and fry the bean curd until golden brown. Drain on paper towels.

● Add the remaining oil to the wok, then fry the garlic and shallots for about 30 seconds. Add the bean sprouts, green beans, and scallions, and stir well.

● Add the bean-thread noodles, bean curd, crushed peanuts, dried shrimp, and green chile, then stir. Season with the sugar, fish sauce, and lemon juice, stirring again.

● Divide the noodles onto four plates. Sprinkle with the crispy onions, cilantro leaves, and red chile, and garnish with lime slices. Serve at once.

Left
Fried Bean-thread Noodles with Bean Curd

Malaysian fried rice noodles

kway teow

If you are ever lucky enough to visit Malaysia, you will find this dish being sold in restaurants and from roadside stalls wherever you go. The fish balls in this recipe are not available at supermarkets, but you should be able to pick them up at oriental food stores.

2 lb fresh flat rice noodles or
  10 oz dried rice-stick noodles
5 tbsp vegetable oil
2 cloves garlic, finely chopped
½-inch piece ginger, peeled and
  minced
6 oz boneless belly of pork or
  chicken breasts, skinned and
  thinly sliced
2 small red chiles, chopped
16 large shrimp with tails,
  peeled and deveined
8 fish balls or portions of
  imitation crabmeat, sliced
3 cups bean sprouts
¼ lb fresh spinach
2 eggs, beaten
1 tsp sugar
3 tbsp light soy sauce
3 tbsp dark soy sauce
salt and black pepper

● Rinse the fresh flat rice noodles with warm water, or soak the dried rice-stick noodles in warm water for 2–5 minutes. Rinse, and drain.

● Heat 3 tablespoons of the oil in a wok or frying pan until very hot. Stir-fry the garlic and ginger for 30 seconds. Add the pork, and fry for about 3 minutes. Add the chile and shrimp, then stir for about a minute. Add the sliced fish balls or crabmeat, the bean sprouts and spinach, and stir again for about a minute.

● Make a well in the center, then add the egg. Scramble quickly. Add the remaining oil, and the rice noodles, sugar, and soy sauce, then stir well. Taste, and add salt and black pepper as required. Put onto four plates, and serve immediately.

Right

Malaysian

Fried Rice

Noodles

noodles with toppings

The concept of this style of noodles is similar to the thinking behind Italian pasta. While you prepare the noodles, you can make the toppings. There are two ways of preparing noodles. They can be boiled like spaghetti, or deep-fried to make them crispy—egg noodles and rice vermicelli are the noodles most commonly deep-fried.

soft noodles with vegetable and peanut sauce

gado gado

Gado gado is one of the most famous Indonesian dishes, comprising vegetables in a peanut sauce. Normally it is served as a salad, but it also makes a great noodle topping!

¼ lb green cabbage, sliced
2½ cups bean sprouts
1 cup green beans
4–5 small carrots, cut into matchsticks
14 oz fresh or 10 oz dried thin egg noodles
1 tbsp sesame oil
For the peanut sauce:
1 tbsp vegetable oil
1 clove garlic, finely chopped
1 shallot, finely chopped
½ tsp chile powder
2¼ cups water
1 tbsp light brown sugar
8 tbsp crunchy peanut butter
a pinch of salt
juice of ½ a lemon

● Heat the oil in a frying pan, and stir-fry the garlic and shallot for 1 minute or until softened. Add the chile powder, water, sugar, and peanut butter, and stir well. Add the salt and lemon juice, stirring again.
● Boil water in a saucepan, and blanch the cabbage, bean sprouts, green beans, and carrots for 2–3 minutes. Drain well.
● Boil more water in the pan, then cook the egg noodles for 3 minutes. Rinse, drain, and toss with the sesame oil. Divide them onto four plates.
● Pile the vegetables on the noodles, and pour the peanut sauce over the top. Serve at once.

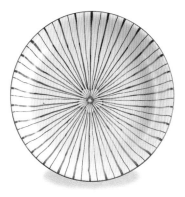

soft egg noodles with ground pork sauce

Toban djan is a fiery Chinese chile bean sauce available from most Chinese or oriental stores, and in a growing number of supermarkets. Here, the power of the chile sauce is tempered by the addition of yellow bean sauce, leaving the dish pleasantly spicy rather than breathtakingly hot.

10 oz dried or 14 oz fresh thin egg noodles
2 tsp sesame oil
For the sauce:
2 tbsp vegetable oil
1 large clove garlic, finely chopped
½-inch piece fresh ginger, peeled and finely chopped
2 scallions, chopped
1 lb ground pork
3 tbsp yellow bean sauce
1 tbsp chile bean sauce (*toban djan*)
2 tbsp Chinese rice wine or dry sherry
2 tbsp dark soy sauce
scant 1 cup chicken stock (*see page 25*) mixed to a paste with 2 tbsp cornstarch
salt and black pepper

● Cook the egg noodles in plenty of boiling water for 3 minutes. Rinse, and drain. Toss in the sesame oil, and divide into four servings.
● Heat the vegetable oil in a pan, and stir-fry the garlic, ginger, and scallions for 30 seconds. Add the ground pork, and fry for 3–4 minutes.
● Add the yellow bean sauce, chile sauce, rice wine, and soy sauce, and stir for 1 minute.
● Add the mixture of stock and cornstarch, and stir until the sauce thickens. Season with salt and black pepper to taste.
● Pour the sauce over the noodles, and serve immediately.

Right
Soft Egg Noodles with Ground Pork Sauce

fried egg noodles with seafood sauce

If you have a taste for slightly richer flavors in this hearty dish, try adding eight abalone to the ingredients.

10 oz dried egg noodles
4 tbsp vegetable oil
1 tbsp sesame oil
1-inch piece fresh ginger, peeled and finely chopped
2 cloves garlic, finely chopped
10 oz squid, cleaned
6 oz peeled jumbo shrimp
4 fish balls or chunks of imitation crabmeat, sliced
9 oz Chinese cabbage, cut into bite-sized squares
salt and white pepper
2½ cups chicken or vegetable stock (see pages 25–26)
1 tbsp Chinese rice wine or dry sherry
3 tbsp cornstarch
4 tbsp water

● Cook the egg noodles in boiling water for 3 minutes. Rinse, and drain. Heat 1 tablespoon of the vegetable oil and sesame oil in a wok or frying pan. Stir-fry the noodles, and put on four plates.
● Heat the remaining vegetable oil in the wok, and stir-fry the ginger and garlic for 30 seconds. Add the squid and shrimp, stirring for 1–2 minutes or until the squid is cooked thoroughly.
● Add the slices of fish ball and Chinese cabbage, sprinkle with salt and white pepper, and stir. Add the stock and rice wine, and bring to a boil. Simmer for 1–2 minutes.
● Combine the cornstarch and water, and add to thicken the sauce. Pour over the noodles, and serve.

fried egg noodles with pork and eggplant sauce

Oyster sauce is a frequently used Chinese flavoring. The surprising thing about oyster sauce is that you would be hard put to find any trace of fishiness in its flavor. It will last for long periods if kept refrigerated, and is widely available from supermarkets.

14 oz fresh or 10 oz dried medium egg noodles
2 tbsp sesame oil
For the sauce:
10 oz boneless belly of pork, skinned and thinly sliced
2½ tbsp light soy sauce
2½ tbsp Chinese rice wine or dry sherry
4 tbsp cornstarch
4 tbsp vegetable oil
1-inch piece fresh ginger, peeled and finely chopped
2 cloves garlic, finely chopped
¾ lb eggplant, sliced into bite-sized pieces and soaked in salted water
4–5 small carrots, sliced
16 canned straw mushrooms, halved
2 scallions, chopped into 1-inch lengths
black pepper
2½ cups chicken stock (see page 25)
2 tbsp oyster sauce
1 tsp sugar
4 tbsp water

● Marinate the pork in 1 tablespoon each of soy sauce, rice wine, and cornstarch. Set aside for 30 minutes, then heat 1 tablespoon of the vegetable oil in a wok or frying pan, and fry the pork for about 3 minutes until lightly browned. Clean the wok.
● Heat the rest of the vegetable oil in the wok until very hot, and stir-fry the ginger and garlic for 30 seconds. Add the drained eggplant and carrots, and stir-fry for a further 1–2 minutes. Add the pork, mushrooms, and scallions, sprinkle black pepper, and stir.
● Add the chicken stock, rice wine, oyster sauce, soy sauce, and sugar, and bring to a boil, simmering for 1 minute. Dissolve the cornstarch in the water and add to thicken the sauce.
● Boil the egg noodles in plenty of water for 4 minutes. Rinse under running water, and drain. Heat the sesame oil in a wok, add the noodles, and quickly stir-fry.
● Divide the egg noodles onto four plates, pour the pork and eggplant sauce over them, then serve at once.

Right

Fried Egg Noodles with Pork and Eggplant

shredded beef and yellow bean sauce on pan-fried egg noodles

Yellow bean sauce is available in two varieties, one using whole beans, the other puréed. The texture differs, but the taste is identical. You can use either in this dish.

1 lb rump steak, shredded
1 tbsp light soy sauce
1 tbsp Chinese rice wine or dry sherry
1 tbsp cornstarch
14 oz fresh or 10 oz dried thin egg noodles
4 tbsp vegetable oil
For the sauce:
2 tbsp vegetable oil
½-inch piece fresh ginger, peeled and finely chopped
4-inch piece leek, cut in half and shredded
3 cups bean sprouts
1 small green pepper, sliced
salt and black pepper
1¾ cups chicken stock
  (see page 25)
6 tbsp whole or puréed yellow bean sauce
1 tbsp light soy sauce
2 tbsp cornstarch
3 tbsp water

● Marinate the beef in the soy sauce, rice wine, and cornstarch for 30 minutes.
● Meanwhile, cook the egg noodles in a pan of boiling water for 3 minutes. Rinse, drain, and divide into four. Heat 1 tablespoon of oil in a wok or frying pan. Take one quarter of the noodles and fry them like a pancake. Press the noodles to form a round, and when they have started to turn golden in color, turn to fry on the other side. Remove to a chopping board, and cut twice in a crisscross pattern to make the noodles easier to eat. Put the noodles on an individual plate. Repeat the process with the other three portions.
● Heat remaining 2 tablespoons of oil in the wok or frying pan; stir-fry the ginger for 30 seconds. Add the leek, bean sprouts, and green pepper, stirring each ingredient as you add it. Sprinkle with salt and pepper.
● Add the chicken stock, yellow bean sauce, and soy sauce; bring to a boil. Combine the cornstarch and water, then add to the sauce, stirring until it thickens. Pour the sauce over the noodles before serving.

Malaysian egg noodles with chicken and shrimp

A Malaysian Chinese dish with a characteristic savory sauce. A typical feature of Malaysian and Singaporean cuisine is the frequent use of egg, as in this dish, in which strands of beaten egg are stirred into the sauce.

14 oz fresh or 10 oz dried thin egg noodles
2 tbsp sesame oil
4 tbsp vegetable oil
2 cloves garlic, finely chopped
¼ lb boneless chicken breasts, sliced into bite-sized pieces
¼ lb peeled shrimp
¼ lb fish balls or imitation crabmeat, sliced
3 cups bean sprouts
¼ lb mustard greens or fresh spinach
1 tsp light soy sauce
1 tsp salt
white pepper
½ tsp sugar
2½ cups chicken stock
  (see page 25)
3 tbsp cornstarch
4 tbsp water
2 eggs, beaten

● Boil plenty of water in a pan, and add the egg noodles. Cook for 3 minutes, then rinse under cold water and drain. Heat the sesame oil in a wok or frying pan, and fry the noodles. Then divide onto four plates.
● Heat the vegetable oil in a wok or frying pan until very hot. Fry the garlic for 30 seconds. Add the chicken and fry for 2–3 minutes. Add the shrimp and stir, then add the fish balls, bean sprouts, and spinach or greens, stirring for 2–3 minutes.
● Add the soy sauce, salt, pepper, sugar, and chicken stock; bring to a boil. Dissolve the cornstarch in water, then add to thicken the sauce. When the sauce returns to the boil, stir in the beaten egg and wait for the egg strands to float up to the surface. Pour the sauce over the noodles, and serve.

Right
Malaysian Egg Noodles with Chicken and Shrimp

sweet and sour fish on pan-fried egg noodles

Sweet and sour fish has never quite gained the same kind of popularity as sweet and sour pork, though it is every bit as good to eat and makes an especially good noodle topping.

vegetable oil for deep-frying
2 tbsp cornstarch
1 egg, beaten
1 tsp water
1 lb cod or haddock steaks, cut into bite-sized pieces
10 oz dried or 14 oz fresh thin egg noodles
4 tbsp vegetable oil
For the sauce:
1 tbsp sesame oil
2 tbsp vegetable oil
1 medium-sized onion, cut into bite-sized squares
1 red pepper, cut into bite-sized squares
½ cup frozen green peas
4-oz can bamboo shoots, cut into halves
10 *shiitake* mushrooms, quartered
½ tsp chile powder
2½ cups chicken stock
  (see page 25)
2½ tbsp sugar
½ cup tomato catsup
4 tsp light soy sauce
4 tbsp Chinese rice wine or dry sherry
4 tbsp vinegar
salt and black pepper
3 tbsp cornstarch
4 tbsp water

● Heat the oil in a pan until very hot. Meanwhile, mix the cornstarch, egg, and water together, then dip the fish in the mixture. Deep-fry for about 2 minutes or until golden brown.
● Cook the egg noodles in plenty of boiling water for 3 minutes. Rinse under running water, drain well, and divide into four. Heat 1 tablespoon of oil in a wok or frying pan. Add a portion of noodles, and press down lightly. Fry until lightly browned, then turn the noodles over, press down lightly, and fry until the other side turns golden brown.
● Put the pan-fried noodles on a chopping board, make a crisscross pattern of cuts, and place on an individual plate. Repeat the process for the other three portions.
● Heat 1 tablespoon sesame oil and 2 tablespoons vegetable oil in the wok or frying pan until very hot. Stir-fry the onion, red pepper, and peas for 2 minutes. Add the bamboo shoots and *shiitake* mushrooms, and sprinkle with the chile powder. Stir-fry for another 2 minutes.
● Add the chicken stock, sugar, tomato catsup, soy sauce, and rice wine, and bring to a boil. Add the vinegar, and season to taste with salt and black pepper.
● Dissolve the cornstarch in the water, and add to thicken the sauce. Add the fish, and stir gently. Pour the sweet and sour fish over the noodles. Serve immediately.

crabmeat sauce on pan-fried egg noodles

10 oz dried or 14 oz fresh medium egg noodles
4 tbsp vegetable oil
For the crabmeat sauce:
2 tbsp vegetable oil
1 clove garlic, finely chopped
½-inch piece fresh ginger, peeled and finely chopped
10 *shiitake* mushrooms, sliced
6 oz canned bamboo shoots, sliced into matchsticks
4 scallions, chopped
¾ lb canned crabmeat
2½ cups water
4 tsp light soy sauce
salt and black pepper
3 tbsp cornstarch
4 tbsp water

● Cook the egg noodles in plenty of water for 4 minutes. Rinse, drain well, and divide into four. Heat 1 tablespoon of oil in a wok or frying pan until very hot. Press one portion of the egg noodles down lightly into the pan and fry until lightly browned on both sides. Place on a chopping board and cut a crisscross pattern. Remove to a plate. Repeat with the three remaining portions.
● Heat 2 tablespoons of oil in the cleaned wok. Fry the garlic and ginger for 30 seconds. Add the *shiitake* mushrooms, bamboo shoots, and scallions, and stir-fry for 1–2 minutes. Add the crabmeat, water, and soy sauce, and season. Bring to a boil, and simmer for 1 minute.
● Dissolve the cornstarch in the water, and add to thicken the sauce. Stir. Pour over the noodles, and serve.

Right
Crabmeat Sauce on Pan-fried Egg Noodles

Thai sweet crispy rice vermicelli

mee krob

Mee krob requires a little more time than most noodle dishes, but is well worth the extra effort. It is essential that the dish is served as soon as it is ready as the vermicelli will become mushy if left for very long.

60 g/2 oz rice vermicelli, slightly crushed
vegetable oil for deep-frying
1 tbsp vegetable oil
2 cloves garlic, finely chopped
2 shallots, finely chopped
12 tiger or jumbo shrimp with tails, peeled and deveined
4 tbsp raw cashew nuts
For the sauce:
3 tbsp palm or brown sugar
2 tbsp freshly squeezed lemon juice
1 tsp vinegar
1 tsp light soy sauce
2 tbsp tomato catsup
½ tsp chile powder
For the garnish:
2 lettuce leaves, halved
cilantro leaves
2 small tomato wedges

● Heat the oil in a wok or saucepan until very hot. Deep-fry the vermicelli for a few seconds until they puff up and become white. Drain on paper towels.

● Heat the oil in the wok or frying pan. Add the garlic and shallots, and stir. Add the shrimp and cashew nuts, and stir-fry for about 2 minutes.

● Add the sugar, lemon juice, vinegar, soy sauce, catsup and chile powder, and simmer until the sauce thickens. Take out the shrimp, and set aside.

● Add the crispy vermicelli, and coat with the sauce. Put the vermicelli on a bed of lettuce on four plates. Garnish each serving with three shrimp, cilantro, and tomato wedges. Serve.

crispy egg noodles with pork sauce

Deep-fried noodles might seem like a strange idea, but, in fact, they are very popular throughout Asia, and make a crunchy and refreshing alternative to boiled noodles.

½ lb dried thin egg noodles
vegetable oil for deep-frying
For the sauce:
½ lb lean pork, sliced on a slant into bite-sized pieces
1 tbsp light soy sauce
4 tbsp cornstarch
8 large dried *shiitake* mushrooms, rinsed
4 tbsp vegetable oil
1-inch piece fresh ginger, peeled and finely chopped
2 cloves garlic, finely chopped
1 medium-sized onion, cut into bite-sized squares
4–5 small carrots, thinly sliced

½ lb Chinese cabbage, cut into bite-sized squares
salt and black pepper
2½ cups chicken stock
(see page 25)
2 tbsp Chinese rice wine or dry sherry
2 tsp sugar
4 tbsp water

● Boil plenty of water in a saucepan, and cook the noodles for 3 minutes. Rinse, and drain. Separate, and spread the noodles on a tray to dry.

● Heat a wok or saucepan a quarter full of oil and heat until very hot. Deep-fry the egg noodles in small batches until golden and crispy. Drain on paper towels.

● Put the pork, soy sauce, and 1 tablespoon of the cornstarch in a bowl, mix, and leave for 15 minutes. Soak the *shiitake* mushrooms in a cup of hot water for 15 minutes, then remove and quarter. Retain the water. Heat 2 tablespoons of the oil in a wok or frying pan, and fry the pork for about 3 minutes. Set aside, and clean the pan.

● Heat 2 tablespoons oil in the wok or pan until very hot. Fry the ginger and garlic for 30 seconds, before adding the onion, carrots, mushrooms, and cabbage. Stir-fry for 2–3 minutes. Add in the meat, season with salt and pepper, and stir.

● Add the water used to soak the mushrooms, plus the chicken stock, rice wine, and sugar; bring to a boil, checking the saltiness.

● Dissolve the remaining 3 tablespoons cornstarch with the water, and add to thicken the sauce. Crush the crispy noodles lightly, and divide onto four plates. Pour the sauce over the noodles, and serve at once.

crispy egg noodles with bean curd and vegetable sauce

This dish is also suitable for vegetarians as I have not used chicken stock. The strong scent of the *shiitake* mushrooms flavors the water, which can be used to add extra aroma to the sauce.

½ lb dried thin egg noodles
vegetable oil for deep-frying
For the sauce:
2 tbsp vegetable oil
1½ lb bean curd (*tofu*)
1 tbsp sesame oil
1-inch piece fresh ginger, peeled
   and finely chopped
2 cloves garlic, finely chopped
8 dried *shiitake* mushrooms,
   rinsed
4-oz can bamboo shoots
4 tbsp frozen green peas
½ lb leek, sliced
4 tsp dark soy sauce
4 tsp light soy sauce
4 tsp yellow bean sauce
½ tsp chile bean sauce
   (*toban djan*)
salt and black pepper
3 tbsp cornstarch mixed with
   4 tbsp water

● Cook the egg noodles in a pan of boiling water for 3 minutes. Rinse, and drain well. Separate and then spread the noodles on a tray to dry. Meanwhile, soak the *shiitake* mushrooms in hot water for 20 minutes, then cut into bite-sized pieces. Retain the water for the stock.

● Fill a wok or pan a quarter full with vegetable oil, and heat to 350°F. Deep-fry the egg noodles in small batches until golden and crispy. Drain on paper towels, and crush lightly.
● Heat 1 tablespoon of the vegetable oil in the wok or frying pan, and fry the bean curd until lightly browned. Drain on paper towels, and clean the wok.
● Heat the remaining tablespoon of vegetable oil and the sesame oil in the wok or pan. Stir-fry the ginger and garlic for 30 seconds, add the mushrooms, bamboo shoots, peas and leek, and stir-fry.
● Make up the soaking water from the mushrooms to 2½ cups, then pour into the wok. Add the soy sauce, yellow bean sauce, and chile bean sauce, and bring to a boil. Season with salt and black pepper if required. Add the cornstarch paste to thicken the sauce. Simmer gently for 1 minute.
● Place the crispy egg noodles onto four plates. Pour the sauce over the top, then serve at once.

chicken and red pepper in egg noodle basket

Noodle baskets are a Chinese innovation that appeal as much to the eyes as to the taste buds. You will need two small sieves about 5 inches across. I find this recipe works best with thinner noodles, and the oil needs to be hot to get nice, crisp, golden baskets. This recipe makes six baskets, which can be presented as a main dish or as a starter with less filling.

½ lb dried thin egg noodles
vegetable oil for deep-frying
For the filling:
6 tbsp vegetable oil
1 lb boneless chicken breasts,
   sliced diagonally into bite-
   sized pieces
salt and black pepper
3 tbsp cornstarch
4 cloves garlic, finely chopped
½-in piece fresh ginger, peeled
   and finely chopped
4-oz can bamboo shoots, sliced
   into matchsticks
⅔ red pepper, diced
4 scallions, chopped
For the sauce:
⅔ cup chicken stock (*see page 25*)
1 tbsp Chinese rice wine or dry
   sherry
1 tbsp light soy sauce
2 tsp dark soy sauce
4 tsp tomato catsup
½ tsp sugar
salt and black pepper
½ tbsp cornstarch
2 tsp water

● Boil the egg noodles for 3 minutes. Rinse with water, drain, separate, and dry on a tray lined with paper towels.

● Heat the oil in a deep pan to 350°F. Oil the sieves, one on the inside, the other on the outside. Line one sieve with egg noodles and press the other sieve down lightly to sandwich them. Carefully deep-fry the noodles with the two sieves holding them together until crispy and golden, about 3–4 minutes. Remove the noodle basket, taking care not to break it. Create five more baskets in the same way.

● Heat 4 tablespoons of oil in a wok or frying pan. Sprinkle the chicken with the salt and pepper, then coat with the cornstarch. Shallow-fry the chicken for 3–4 minutes, or until golden brown. Drain on paper towels.

● Heat the remaining 2 tablespoons of oil in the wok, stir-fry the garlic and ginger, then add the bamboo, red pepper, and onion. Stir well. Add the chicken stock, rice wine, soy sauce, catsup, and sugar, bring to a boil, and season if required.

● Combine the cornstarch and water, then add to thicken the sauce. Return the chicken to the pan, and stir. Place the noodle baskets on six plates, and fill with the chicken mixture. Serve at once.

Left
Chicken and Red Pepper in Egg Noodle Basket

crispy egg noodles with chicken and bean sprout sauce

Take care when preparing the noodles for this dish, as the oil may boil over if an excessive amount is used. The best and safest method is to use a wok rather than a frying pan.

½ lb dried medium egg noodles
vegetable oil for deep-frying
1 egg white
2 tsp cornstarch
6 tbsp vegetable oil
10 oz boneless chicken breasts, shredded
For the sauce:
1 tbsp sesame oil
2 cloves garlic, finely chopped
1-inch piece fresh ginger, peeled and finely chopped
14 oz bean sprouts
15 canned straw mushrooms, halved
4 scallions, chopped
2½ cups chicken stock
  (see page 25)
2 tsp light soy sauce
2 tbsp Chinese rice wine or dry sherry
salt and black pepper
3 tbsp cornstarch
4 tbsp water

● Boil plenty of water in a pan, and cook the noodles for 4 minutes. Rinse, and drain. Separate, and then spread the noodles on a tray to dry.

● Fill a saucepan or wok quarter full of oil and heat to 350°F. Deep-fry the noodles in small batches until golden and crispy. Drain on paper towels. Crush the noodles lightly to make them easier to handle, and divide onto three plates.

● Mix the egg white and 2 teaspoons of cornstarch. Heat 5 tablespoons of the vegetable oil in the wok or frying pan. Coat the chicken with the cornstarch mixture, then shallow-fry until golden brown. Discard the oil, and clean the wok or pan.

● Heat the remaining tablespoon of vegetable oil and the sesame oil in the wok until very hot. Stir-fry the garlic and ginger for 30 seconds. Add the bean sprouts, mushrooms, and scallions, then stir-fry for 2 minutes.

● Return the chicken to the wok, then add the stock, soy sauce, and rice wine. Season with salt and black pepper. Bring to a boil, and simmer for 1–2 minutes.

● Dissolve the cornstarch in the water, then add to thicken the sauce. Pour the sauce over the noodles just prior to eating.

crispy rice vermicelli with shredded chicken

You will be surprised at the rapid expansion of the vermicelli the first time you try this dish. The key is to deep-fry it in small amounts to prevent it from overflowing from your wok or pan. The noodles are ready when they have lost their transparency and have turned white.

¼ lb rice vermicelli
vegetable oil for deep-frying
For the sauce:
1 lb boneless chicken breasts, shredded
2 tbsp light soy sauce
2 tbsp Chinese rice wine or dry sherry
3 tbsp cornstarch
4 tbsp vegetable oil
1-inch piece fresh ginger, peeled and finely chopped
8 *shiitake* mushrooms, shredded
12 water chestnuts, sliced
4 scallions, chopped into 1-inch lengths
salt and black pepper
1¾ cups chicken stock
  (see page 25)
1 tsp sesame oil
1 tbsp tomato catsup
½ tsp sugar
3 tbsp water
6 lettuce leaves, rinsed and quartered

● Fill a wok or saucepan a quarter full of vegetable oil, and heat to 350°F. Deep-fry the rice vermicelli in small batches at a time. It will puff up in seconds. Drain on paper towels.

● Marinate the chicken in 1 tablespoon each of the soy sauce, rice wine, and cornstarch for 30 minutes. Heat 2 tablespoons of oil in a wok or frying pan, and fry the chicken for 3–4 minutes. Set aside.

● Heat the remaining 2 tablespoons of the vegetable oil in the wok. Add the ginger and stir-fry for 30 seconds. Add the *shiitake* mushrooms, water chestnuts, scallions, and chicken, sprinkle with salt and pepper, then stir-fry for 1–2 minutes.

● Add the chicken stock, sesame oil, tomato catsup, sugar, and remaining soy sauce and rice wine, and bring to a boil. Combine the remaining

cornstarch and water, then add to thicken the sauce. Stir well.

● To serve, pile the lettuce leaves onto a small plate. Put the crispy vermicelli onto four individual plates, and pour the chicken sauce over the top. When you eat, take one lettuce leaf and wrap some noodles and chicken sauce together in a bundle, then pop it into your mouth.

Right
Crispy Rice
Vermicelli
with
Shredded
Chicken

beef and celery on crispy vermicelli

The steak used in this dish should be very lean and cut small enough for it to absorb the flavors of the marinade, which contains vinegar to soften the meat before cooking.

1 lb rump steak, sliced diagonally into bite-sized pieces
1 tsp vinegar
2 tsp light soy sauce
1 egg white
5 oz rice vermicelli
vegetable oil for deep-frying
4 tbsp vegetable oil
2 cloves garlic, finely chopped
1-inch piece fresh ginger, peeled and finely chopped
3 scallions, chopped
8 stalks celery, sliced diagonally
4-oz can bamboo shoots
For the sauce:
1¾ cups chicken stock
  (see page 25)
1 tbsp light soy sauce
1 tbsp Chinese rice wine or dry sherry
2 tsp oyster sauce
2 tbsp cornstarch mixed to a paste with 3 tbsp water

● Marinate the beef in the vinegar, soy sauce, and egg white for 30 minutes.
● Fill a wok or saucepan a quarter full of oil and heat to 350°F. Deep-fry the vermicelli for a few seconds in small batches until they puff up. Drain on paper towels, then arrange on four plates. Crush lightly.
● Heat 2 tablespoons of the oil in a wok or frying pan. Stir-fry the beef until golden brown. Clean the pan.

● Heat the remaining 2 tablespoons of the oil in the wok. Stir-fry the garlic, ginger, scallions, celery, and bamboo shoots for 2 minutes. Return the beef to the pan, and stir well.
● Add the chicken stock, soy sauce, rice wine, and oyster sauce, then heat for 2 minutes. Stir in the combined cornstarch paste to thicken the sauce. Pour the sauce over the crispy vermicelli, and serve immediately.

crispy vermicelli with chicken and mango

A modern Chinese dish that looks set to become a great favorite. Fried vermicelli must be eaten as quickly as possible once it is ready.

5 oz rice vermicelli
vegetable oil for deep frying
1 egg white
3⅔ tbsp cornstarch
1 lb boneless chicken breasts, sliced into bite-sized pieces
salt and black pepper
4 tbsp vegetable oil
2 cloves garlic, finely chopped
1-inch piece fresh ginger, peeled and finely chopped
3 stalks celery, sliced diagonally
1 medium-sized onion, cubed
1 mango, cut into bite-sized pieces
2½ cups chicken stock
  (see page 25)
2 tbsp Chinese rice wine or dry sherry
3 tbsp light soy sauce
2½ tbsp sugar
4 tbsp water

● Fill a wok or saucepan a quarter full of oil, and heat to 350°F. Deep-fry the vermicelli in small batches only a few seconds until they turn white. Drain on paper towels.
● Mix the egg white and 2 teaspoons of the cornstarch in a bowl. Sprinkle the chicken with salt and black pepper, and coat with the cornstarch mixture.
● Heat 2 tablespoons of the oil in a wok or frying pan until very hot. Fry the chicken for about 2 minutes. When finished, discard the oil and clean the pan.
● Heat the remaining 2 tablespoons of oil in the wok. Stir-fry the garlic and ginger for 30 seconds before adding the celery, onion, and chicken. Stir-fry for 2–3 minutes.
● Add the chicken stock, rice wine, soy sauce, and sugar, then bring to a boil. Add the mango, season with salt and black pepper, and simmer for 1–2 minutes. Combine the remaining cornstarch with the water, and add to thicken the sauce.
● Divide the crispy vermicelli onto four plates, and lightly crush. Pour the sauce over the top just before serving.

sweet and sour pork on crispy vermicelli

Perhaps the most popular Chinese dish in the west. It is equally at home with noodles as with rice.

5 oz rice vermicelli
vegetable oil for deep-frying
I lb boneless belly of pork, skinned and cut into bite-sized pieces
I tbsp Chinese rice wine or dry sherry
I tbsp light soy sauce
3 tbsp cornstarch
I egg white
4–5 carrots, cut at random into bite-sized pieces
2 tbsp vegetable oil
I tbsp sesame oil
I medium-sized onion, cut into bite-sized pieces
I green pepper, cut into bite-sized squares
For the sauce:
1¾ cups chicken stock
  (see page 25)
2⅔ tbsp sugar
½ cup tomato catsup
1⅓ tbsp light soy sauce
4 tbsp Chinese rice wine or dry sherry
4 tbsp vinegar
salt and black pepper
2 tbsp cornstarch
3 tbsp water

● Fill a wok or saucepan a quarter full of oil, and heat to 350°F. Separate the vermicelli into small portions. Deep-fry the vermicelli in several batches in the wok. They puff up in a few seconds, so be ready to take them out promptly. Drain on paper towels. Put the crispy vermicelli onto four plates, and lightly crush.

● Marinate the pork in the rice wine and soy sauce for 20–30 minutes. Mix 2 tablespoons of the cornstarch, the egg white, and I teaspoon of water together in a bowl, and coat the pork with the cornstarch mixture. Deep-fry the meat for about 4–5 minutes, or until golden brown. Drain on paper towels, then crush lightly and arrange on four plates.

● Cook the carrots in a pan of boiling water for about 15 minutes, then set aside. Heat I tablespoon vegetable oil and I tablespoon sesame oil in the wok or frying pan until very hot. Stir-fry the onion and green pepper for 1–2 minutes, add the carrots, and stir for a further minute.

● Add the chicken stock, sugar, tomato catsup, soy sauce, and rice wine, and bring to a boil. Add the vinegar, and season.

● Combine the cornstarch with the water, and stir well into the sauce. Add the pork. Scoop the sweet and sour pork onto the noodles, and serve immediately.

pork and pineapple in honey sauce on crispy vermicelli

Another dish with a sweet and sour theme. The honey and pineapple complement the pork very well.

5 oz rice vermicelli
vegetable oil for deep-frying
I lb boneless belly of pork, skinned and cut into bite-sized pieces
salt and black pepper
I tbsp Chinese rice wine or dry sherry
2½ tbsp cornstarch
2 tbsp water
For the sauce:
2 tbsp vegetable oil
I-inch piece fresh ginger, peeled and finely chopped
I clove garlic, finely chopped
2 medium-sized onions, cubed
4–5 carrots, sliced
4 pineapple rings (canned), chopped
salt and black pepper
1¾ cups chicken stock
  (see page 25)
2 tbsp honey
2 tsp brown sugar
I tsp light soy sauce
4 tbsp pineapple juice (from the can)
2 tbsp cornstarch mixed with 3 tbsp water

● Fill a wok or saucepan a quarter full of vegetable oil, and heat to 350°F. Deep-fry the rice vermicelli in small batches. They will puff up in a few seconds. Drain on paper towels.

● Sprinkle the pork with salt and black pepper, then marinate in the rice wine for 15 minutes. Combine the cornstarch and water, and coat the pork with the paste. Deep-fry the pork until lightly browned. Drain on paper towels.

● Heat the oil in the cleaned wok or frying pan. Stir-fry the ginger and garlic for 30 seconds. Add the onions and carrots, and stir-fry for about 2 minutes. Add the pineapple, lightly sprinkle with salt and pepper, and stir.

● Add chicken stock, honey, sugar, soy sauce, and pineapple juice. When the sauce is boiling, add the combined cornstarch and water to thicken the sauce. Add the pork, and mix.

● Put the crispy vermicelli onto four plates, then lightly crush. Pour on sauce, and serve immediately.

Left

Sweet and Sour Pork on Crispy Vermicelli

Index